THE WORLD IS NOT ENOUGH

THE WORLD
IS NOT ENOUGH

A COMPANION

IAIN JOHNSTONE

This edition published in 1999 by Boxtree,
an imprint of Macmillan Publishers Ltd,
25 Eccleston Place, London, SW1W 9NF, Basingstoke and Oxford

Associated companies throughout the world

ISBN 0 7522 1799 2

9 8 7 6 5 4 3 2 1

A CIP catalogue record for this book is available from the British Library

Design by Jane Coney

Printed in Great Britain by The Bath Press, Bath

CONTENTS

PREFACE

When the gifted cinematographer David Watkin won an Oscar and innumerable international prizes for his work on *Out of Africa*, he told me that every time he walked up to the podium at an awards ceremony they would play the lyical John Barry theme and show an accompanying shot of graceful pink flamingoes flying into the sunset. What was interesting about this footage was that Watkin had nothing whatsoever to do with it – it was taken by some aerial wildlife unit.

If fellow professionals have difficulty in disentangling who did what on a big movie, is it little wonder that critics and commentators make mistakes? In my time as *The Sunday Times* Film Critic I'm sure I've praised a writer for a actor's ad lib or a director for a sequence choreographed by the camera operator.

So I had an appetite to write a book that might clarify matters a little. More than a thousand people worked on *The World Is Not Enough*. This account is not a job sheet for each one of them but it attempts to give some insight into the way the cake was divided up, from uncredited writers to added laboratory inserts – although the Bond films are unique in their determination to make the Computer Generated Image the last resort. When someone falls from a cliff top, the odds are somebody is doing it for real.

My thanks to Barbara Broccoli and Michael Wilson for giving me unrestricted access to their movie, especially generous of them since when people read this book they will know exactly how to make a Bond film themselves providing they have a) the rights to the character and b) about $100 million.

Adrian Biddle and his crew made me more than welcome on the set, all of them anxious to reminisce about the long hot summer of *Fierce Creatures*.

Michael Apted, whom I first met on *Agatha* when Vanessa Redgrave was trying to sell a pro-Palestinian newspaper to Dustin

Hoffman, permitted me to share his philosophy of "007 Up." And Pierce Brosnan was happy to have me watch him at work, even when he was in bed with Denise Richards.

My thanks go to Keith Hamshere and Jay Maidment for the exquisite accuracy of their photography; all opinions and inaccuracies in the text are unreservedly mine.

Iain Johnstone
London
September 1999

The Author and the Agent.

INTRODUCTION

ELEKTRA:

I could have given you the world.

BOND:

The world is not enough.

ELEKTRA:

Foolish sentiment.

BOND:

Family motto.

Although the Bond producers may have run out of the works of Ian Fleming (who wrote the 12 Bond novels and two short stories) for the plot of their nineteenth film, the author nevertheless provided them with a title. It comes from *On Her Majesty's Secret Service*. 007 has to visit the College of Arms to investigate Ernst Stavro Blofeld's (bogus) claim to the title of Count. He intends to gain access to Blofeld's Swiss lair by pretending to be a member of the College, Sir Hilary Bray. A genealogist looks up Sir Thomas Bond's actual family crest which has three bezants (roundels) and the motto 'The World Is Not Enough'. In the 1969 movie (with George Lazenby as Bond) his motto is formally referred to in Latin: 'Orbis Non Suffict.' But Latin titles don't go down too well at the international box office nowadays, so it is the motto's translation that will be further translated into numerous languages across the globe.

In the beginnning Cubby Broccoli and Harry Salzman based their films fairly faithfully on Ian Fleming's novels. Then, using the title of the short stories – *The Living Daylights* and *Octopussy* – Broccoli took a little poetic licence and by the time he named a film after Fleming's house in Jamaica, *Goldeneye*, total licence. But the Fleming template is still what we expect from a Bond film and *The World Is Not Enough* is no exception. 007 is given an assignment by the head of MI6, M, to track down an international villain (who is frequently hell-bent on world domination or destruction). He already has a licence to kill and the disapproving Q will give him some state-of-the art weapons and other aids that will prove opportunely useful. On his journey Bond will certainly enjoy some women, some vodka-martinis and maybe a night at a casino before he invariably finds himself the captive of the maniac he has been sent to capture. Does he escape and reverse the roles? I think we know – just as we know there will be a twentieth James Bond film.

The audience would feel deprived if the movie did not include most or all of these elements – Bond movies are as strictly traditional as Japanese Noh plays, or indeed *Dr No* movies. But the art of the film-makers is to combine the conventional structure with a wholly original and inventive adventure that will satisfy audience anticipation.

How do they manage that? It takes talent. Not just one talent – abundant talent. A first, second, model and sometimes third unit with multiple cameras filmed from January to June 1999 to put the picture in the can.

Bond is the longest-running cinema franchise in the world. The first film, *Dr No*, was released in autumn 1962. Thus the series has run for more than a third of the life of cinema itself. So they must be doing something right.

But what? I was permitted access to the stars and sets of this latest movie and talked to key people in front of and behind camera in a quest to find out exactly that.

CHAPTER ONE

CREATING BROSNAN'S BOND

I t would be incorrect to give the impression that the Bond films have
formed an unbroken upward graph of increasing praise and
profitability as the years have gone by. Bond films tend to make most
of their profits internationally, but the second Timothy Dalton film,
Licence To Kill (1989) was not sucessful in the core US market It
took only $35 million. In terms of action and adventure it was rich
enough, with big sequences on land, sea and air, and Dalton certainly
brought a credible intensity to the part. But something was missing. It
wasn't quite Bond. The villain had no world-dominating ambitions
other than running drugs. The art of the Bond series has always been
to change with the times and somehow this one seemed to be a beat
behind. Had Indiana Jones taken over the mantle of droll man
of action?

The Chinese ideogram for 'crisis' is the same as the one for
'opportunity' and this proved to be the case with the Bond films. The
father of the series, Cubby Broccoli, was locked in litigation with
MGM/UA about the sale of the Bond library to television and video.
So after 16 films in 27 years, there was an unprecedented gap of six
years before the next Bond came out. In that time Broccoli sadly
contracted his final illness but, with Timothy Dalton feeling it was
time to do other things after the prolonged break, Cubby was able to
cast the man whom he had originally wanted to succeed Roger Moore
– Pierce Brosnan.

And around this time something happened. Barbara Broccoli,
Cubby's daughter and now co-producer of the series with her
stepbrother, Michael G. Wilson, modestly attributes it to three men:
Pierce Brosnan himself; Martin Campbell, the director of *GoldenEye*;
and Bruce Feirstein, one of the writers. They evolved a new Bond for
the nineties who was to prove very much in chime with public taste.
Brosnan as Bond twice topped the $100-million mark at the US box

Producer Michael Wilson with Sophie Marceau.

office and *GoldenEye* and *Tomorrow Never Dies* brought in grosses of $800 million around the world.

So as we look at the third film in this trilogy, *The World Is Not Enough*, one central question must be: what was the magic touch?

As with any such alchemy, nobody is absolutely sure which element it was. In truth, it was probably a propitious combination. But what all three men had in common was a hunger – they were desperate to reinvent the wheel. Martin Campbell had made a name in television with *Edge of Darkness*, but his career in feature films was restricted to the well-received but not widely seen prison-ship film, *No Escape*. Bruce Feirstein was better known for his book *Real Men Don't Eat Quiche* than for films based on his screenplays.

But the hungriest of the three was Brosnan. He had a well-established television career with *Remington Steele* and *The Last Of*

The Mohicans but his film work in *Mrs Doubtfire* and *The Fourth Protocol* and even the popular *The Lawnmower Man* rarely gave him an opportunity to explore his range.

Having been offered but having had to turn down the role of Bond in 1986 because of his television contract, he had been given a second chance and he felt that fate had intended it. But he sensed the burden of the enterprise on his shoulders and it made him very nervous. 'Terror, more like,' he told me:

I didn't have any chances. There was a lot at stake. I didn't want to be the man who put the final nail in the coffin. If I screwed up and it hadn't worked, I don't know if the series would have gone on. Tim gave a wonderful performance, a performance which was very true to what Fleming had put down. But the world, the punters, the audience had been conditioned and

primed with humour and a kind of sly nod to the audience. If you're going to play it dead straight and on the nose, then it had better be rich in many varying aspects of the character. The audience want to have fun.

Brosnan knew that he was working with the right man in Campbell. 'I was served really well with Martin. He paid attention to the detail, to the style, to the cinematic workings of this particular movie. It had to be goosed and goosed well because the competition in the market was so big.'

Michael Wilson, himself a co-writer of four Bonds and an uncredited collaborator in subsequent ones, has always been gently amused that such a quintessential New Yorker as Bruce Feirstein should be the man to get inside the mind of the archetypal British naval commander. Feirstein made an early inroad into the 'macho man' territory with his '*Quiche*' book and it probably took an outsider to finger the idiosyncrasies of James Bond.

Feirstein insists:

Much as everyone would like to go back to the early Bond films, that character wouldn't work today. That character wouldn't exist. You can't be that sexist, for a start. But what I think Pierce brought to the screen in a wonderful way is the inner conflict – the conflict of someone who can get up in the morning and have to kill someone by sundown. Someone who has lived a life. It's reflected in his attitude. You get a sense of the tragedy of Bond's inner life, which is that he's an adult yet he's someone who can't have long-term relationships for fear that he could end up dead tomorrow. I think Pierce reflects that. Pierce isn't as dark as Timothy. He's not as frothy as Roger Moore. He is a unique Bond that is different from Connery. It was strange on *GoldenEye* – before I met Pierce, I heard Connery's voice as I wrote. I only hear Pierce now.

Brosnan was aware that with Campbell setting the style and piling on the action, and with Feirstein's attention to character and addition of a nice sprinkling of wit, he had to cut a direct and sympathetic line as the new Bond. 'I kept it as straight and as simple as I possibly could. The one thing that had been lacking was the humour and now the humour is there. Not overdone on my behalf but nevertheless the humour is there and, as well as that, I think, an enjoyment of the role.'

The best dramatic humour tends to come out of conflict and a new seam was mined by making M a woman. It was actually Martin Campbell's idea. At 6 o'clock one morning, just before shooting, he gave an early draft to Feirstein and asked: 'What do you think of the M scene?' The American replied: 'It's a bunch of white guys sitting around talking.'

So Campbell suggested: 'Well, why don't you try it as a woman?' By 11 a.m. M had changed sex, but, more than that, a new combative element arose that defined both characters.

On the surface they appear to be wholly at odds with each other. M says that Bond thinks she's a 'bean counter who's more interested in my numbers than your instincts' and Bond doesn't disagree. And M accuses him of being 'a sexist, misogynist dinosaur – a relic of the Cold War'.

Neither remark is really meant – we know that deep down they respect each other. But the way the game was played, far from making Bond a dinosaur, brought a new warmth and genuine concern into their relationship. From now on M had an almost maternal concern for Bond's safety. And this built the foundation for heightened emotion in *The World Is Not Enough*, where, in a complete reversal, it is suddenly M's life that is in jeopardy and Bond who must come to her aid. If it is a British characteristic to be economical with emotions,

then this is raised to an art form by officers of MI6. Thus the tradi-
tionally flip dialogue of the Bond films can mask much less flip
emotions. This is a superior form of screenwriting and is a particularly
satisfactory style of storytelling.

One of the most significant decisions of the Brosnan Bonds and one
which blended the elements of adventure, action and character into an
appealing whole was to pinpoint the era in which the story takes place.

Bruce Feirstein quotes Cubby Broccoli: 'The Bond films are set
five minutes into the future. You can do anything that is possible with
existing technology which you can throw an unlimited amount of
money at. You can't time-travel, you can't clone human beings, you
can't travel faster than the speed of light. These things are for *Star
Wars* or *Star Trek*.'

Pierce Brosnan in front of a wind machine on location in Spain.

Michael Wilson sees this as a fundamental rule:

It's not a science-fiction film. All the technology in the film is presently available although maybe in reality nobody could devote enough money, time or effort into doing some of the things these characters get up to. But nothing is impossible in any physical sense, so it's not a science-fiction film. The hero goes on a quest to different locations in a contemporary action-adventure film that takes place in a world that is parallel to our own but not quite the same. Things are a little more sophisticated and exotic, the women are more beautiful, the villains are much nastier. There's a kind of hyper-reality to it.

But however inventive the technology or lush the locations or perverted the villains, the pivot on which a Bond film balances is the man himself. For a global audience in the nineties Brosnan is Bond. But to what extent is Bond Brosnan? I talked to Pierce about this, thinking it must be a familiar enquiry, but he took his time and pondered the point thoughtfully.

'I think there is a physicality in playing Bond which has to be there and I don't think I carry that in real life. He is a Commander, he has a commanding presence when he enters a room or is dealing with people, he's a man who's used to wearing uniform. More than that, his body language is that of a survivor.'

Brosnan's natural voice has more than a hint of his Irish childhood in it, but for Bond he assumes a tone that is eloquently classless and which has the low pitch of a man who does not need to raise his voice to establish his authority.

Some time after my question, he voluntarily came back to the subject of when Brosnan becomes Bond. He said he thought it was most probably when he arrived at the studio in the morning.

'You come in, you put on the suit and you're there. I never have a conversation for more than four minutes on the set so I'm usually just in my own space, in my own time zone. There's a certain attitude and energy and formality to the body that comes into being without you even knowing.'

Paul Taylor, the second assistant director, and Christopher Brosnan, the third assistant and Pierce's stepson, had come to collect him for his next shot. They set off along the wide corridors of Pinewood towards G Stage. Few, if any, words were spoken. Brosnan's bearing became upright and dignified, his look was purposeful but vigilant, his pace military and determined. As he walked towards the Bond set, the character seemed to come towards him.

CHAPTER TWO

FINDING THE PLOT

The primary idea for *The World Is Not Enough* came from Barbara Broccoli. *GoldenEye* had been such a phenomenal hit in 1995, and MGM/UA had such confidence that *Tomorrow Never Dies* (1997) would be just as big that, even before the latter opened, the pressure was back on her and Michael Wilson to produce a new Bond movie every two years.

As Barbara says, when you know you're looking for an original plot, everything with any potential that you read or hear on the radio or see on television is absorbed with this in mind. In the case of *The World Is Not Enough* the inspiration came on a plane. She was flying to Miami just after the opening of *Tomorrow Never Dies*. Part of the in-flight entertainment was a recording of an edition of Ted Koppel's *Nightline* broadcast by ABC on 13 November 1997.

This was devoted to the Caspian Sea and had the Pulitzer Prize-winning writer Daniel Yergin stating that Caspian Sea oil may help determine no less than global economic growth in the next century. During the 70 years that the Caspian was under the control of the Soviet Union the vast oilfields – estimated at anywhere from 40 to 200 billion barrels – were an underused asset. The Russians didn't like deep-sea drilling, erecting a vast network of shallow-water walkways 30 miles offshore but still preferring to get most of their oil from Siberia.

Since the collapse of the USSR, Baku, capital of the independent Muslim state of Azerbaijan, has become the centre of the world's last great oil boom. Every major oil company in the world is now there. What was once an impoverished backwater town has now the trappings of fast Western wealth: five-star hotels, crowded casinos and numerous happy millionaires.

Drilling for oil in the Caspian Sea is relatively uncomplicated with modern technology. The problem lies in getting the oil out of the area. Nearly every projected pipeline has to go through some politically turbulent state. What if someone was so utterly ruthless as to destroy all the opposition and make sure their pipeline was the only conduit for the 'black gold' to reach the West? What would you call a maniac like that? A Bond villain, perhaps?

If anybody had a nose for a potential Bond story, Barbara Broccoli had. She was reared on them, having had the good sense to be born shortly before the first one, *Dr No*, went into production. She worked

Producer Barbara Broccoli checks playback with second unit director Vic Armstrong.

as an assistant director on two Roger Moore Bonds and, when Roger stepped down, was actually dispatched to Australia to look for possible replacements. She was line producer on the Timothy Dalton duo and then took over the role of co-producer with Michael Wilson, with their mother, Dana Broccoli, still very much involved. Determined to assert her independence from the family firm, she bought the rights to the Ludovic Kennedy book about the Lindbergh Kidnapping – *The Airman and the Carpenter* – and turned it into the Emmy-nominated HBO film, *Crime of the Century.*

Barbara, although attractive and articulate, with a vocabulary that can be hard-hitting if she wants to get her point home, genuinely eschews the limelight – she leaves that for the stars. When television crews and journalists come to the Bond set, any comments from the producers are very much Michael's province.

Michael, Dana Broccoli's son by a previous marriage, was practising as an international lawyer in 1973 when Cubby asked him to take a sabbatical and come to London to help sort out problems he had with the Inland Revenue and also his partner, Harry Saltzman. He handled both tasks with sufficient success to find himself integrated in the family business – as an executive producer, a writer and, starting with *A View To A Kill* (1985), co-producer with his stepfather. It would be his natural constituency to run the business side of Danjaq but he once told me that he voluntarily demoted himself so that he could remain at the creative end of the movies. Nobody doubts, however, his power to pull the strings if necessary.

Wilson is a quietly spoken man, his dress and demeanour very much those of an academic. Unlike Cubby, nothing about him is flamboyant. But he and his wife, Jane, are very much keepers of the Bond conscience. Nothing is licensed to thrill under the Bond banner without his considered permission.

He also has a good sense of humour. 'How would you define your working relationship with Barbara?' I asked him. 'I do whatever she tells me,' he came back with a poker face – followed by a broad grin.

He liked Barbara's idea for a potential plot and both of them liked the work of the British writers Neal Purvis and Robert Wade that their development executive, Simon Mathew, had brought to their attention. The two men had written *Let Him Have It* (1991), the story of the Craig-Bentley case, in which a British policeman was murdered, and their screenplay for the forthcoming highwayman movie, *Plunkett And Macleane*, was attracting attention in Hollywood.

The two men, now in their mid-thirties, who met when they were students at the University of Kent at Canterbury, got a call from their agent telling them to go along to meet the producers at Eon Productions, the Bond HQ in Piccadilly. Eon House is a tall and imposing Georgian building. I have always felt that it had the air of an embassy

Writers Neal Purvis and Robert Wade.

but Neal Purvis's first impression was that it looked like a Bond villain's office.

After a general discussion about their work, Michael Wilson asked them casually: 'So what do you think James Bond should do next?' It was not a question they had applied themselves to, so Purvis said that he would quite like to see what Bond had been doing at home and what his place was like and Wade joked that it might be in need of redecoration with him being away so much.

The humour rather than the suggestion endeared them to the producers. Although in the books Fleming makes much of Bond's Chelsea apartment and his housekeeper, May, in the movies 007 is like the Man With No Name – he comes from nowhere and returns to nowhere.

It was agreed they would meet again in a couple of weeks to discuss ideas. Barbara subsequently showed them a tape of the ABC

Nightline programme. The writers could see the potential in the oil boom, with its vital pipelines and Caspian Sea walkways. They suggested the idea of integrating a caviar factory in the set-up and thus the scene began to be set.

Over the next months in London and Los Angeles the writers sat with the producers and Simon Mathew and batted around ideas. Purvis and Wade knew that the most important new character in any Bond movie is the villain. They thought it might be original to have a villain who was dead, but acknowledged that this might present problems in the traditional final fight with Bond. So a compromise was reached. Renard (French for 'fox') would have a bullet lodged in his skull, in the medulla oblongata (the focal point of the central nervous system – 'That's the beauty of having the Encyclopaedia Britannica on a CD-ROM,' Purvis observed). This would mean that he was slowly dying as opposed to dead and that he would actually become stronger, as he would feel less and less pain as the end approached.

Purvis also wanted a female villain since he felt there had never been a full-blown one in a Bond film before. Maud Adams as the eponymous Octopussy in 1983 was ostensibly the owner of a travelling circus but was in fact a gem smuggler in partnership with Kamal Khan (played by Louis Jordan). But she turns good well before the end of the film and helps Bond to thwart a more nefarious piece of nuclear-bomb smuggling. The writers studied previous Bond films – they appreciated the luxury of being able to view Dana's Broccoli's own prints in MGM's private cinema – and found some clues in the character of Tracy di Vicenzo in *On Her Majesty's Secret Service* (1969). Played by Diana Rigg, she is the spoiled daughter of the boss of Europe's major crime syndicate. She, like Octopussy, finds redemption – followed by marriage to 007 and, unfortunately, death – before the end of the film.

Wade said she was a very strong inspiration for the character of Elektra in *The World Is Not Enough*, because she is a rich man's daughter who is out to prove herself and Bond is on a mission to look after this girl, whom he at first finds vulnerable and then not so vulnerable.

The other new female character in the film is Christmas Jones. Wade recalls:

She was originally a Polynesian girl who worked for Lloyds of London South Seas Bureau. Actually it probably doesn't exist but we thought it sounded good. We took the name Christmas from Christmas Humphreys, who was the prosecutor in the Craig and Bentley case and was the first person who popularized Buddhism in England. Christmas was a paperwork girl, not an action girl, but she was on the same trail as Bond. But the first treatment came back from the studio, UA, who asked us to make her something other than an insurance investigator as they'd just okayed Pierce to make *The Thomas Crown Affair* and the lead woman in that is an insurance investigator. So Christmas briefly became a bounty hunter and ended up as a nuclear expert.

Michael Wilson had long wanted to see if there was a chance to use a helicopter tree saw in a Bond movie. This looks like a giant vertical chain-saw and is used in Canada for cutting down inaccessible branches of huge trees that are interfering with cable lines. The idea had been mooted for *GoldenEye* but had not made it to the final draft. Here, however, it was the ideal instrument for an attack on the wooden Baku walkways and Purvis and Wade capped it with a gag from an old Laurel and Hardy movie in which a car is sawn in half – in this case, Bond's brand-new BMW Z8.

Wilson went on location recces to Baku and Istanbul. Eon set up a website which the writers could access with a password so that the producer could put a series of digital photos on it for them to download so that they could see the places that they were considering filming and could then write for those locations.

The writers told the bare bones of the story to Pierce Brosnan at a meal in Los Angeles. Purvis said how they wanted the film to be more Hitchcockian than the other Bonds and not just have Bond running around with a machine-gun. This had worked well enough at the end of *Tomorrow Never Dies*, but when you're at a distance spraying bullets, Purvis suggested, you have no contact with the other characters.

Goldie takes tea with director Michael Apted.

Brosnan responded to this. He said he really wanted to go to work on people, in scenes where he gets his face really into their face.

A version of the script was completed before Michael Apted was appointed director in August 1998. He liked the idea of M being more involved in the plot than usual and encouraged the writers to do a feasibility study of her going out on a mission herself, because of a personal involvement with Elektra. This had been established early in the script and, knowing what an expert actress he had in Judi Dench as M, Apted wanted to play to this strength. 'The script had a lot of strong elements but still didn't quite make sense,' he said. 'The biggest thing that came into play at that time was the kidnapping of M, which beefed up the back story and beefed up the whole thing.'

'Michael made us focus more on scenes between people rather than things, as that kept the story moving forward,' Wade remembered. 'At the same time we were in quite an interesting position, which we had never been involved in before, where a set [for a nuclear facility] was being constructed before you've rewritten the sequence that is actually going to happen in it.'

Apted still wanted more work on the character of Elektra. He felt the film would only work if her relationship with Bond worked. The studio suggested that the director's wife, Dana Stevens, who had written *City Of Angels* and more recently *The Love Game*, starring Kevin Costner, would be the ideal person to do this.

It's almost the norm in pictures of this size to customize the writers for certain elements. There seemed to be no hard feelings as Purvis and Wade handed over to Dana Stevens. They had laid down the bedrock plot and it was indicated to them that they would be welcome aboard the next Bond film.

Miss Stevens worked for just three weeks, during which time she did two drafts, restructuring Elektra and the climax between her and M. Apted explained to me:

We then realized we had to go further, suddenly Bond was second banana here and Elektra and M were taking over the film. So Bruce Feirstein came back and brought something quite different to it. He rewrote the Bond scenes basically and put Bond in his proper place. In the last Bond they had had a lot of trouble with the script, largely because, there had been so much conflict. They had people coming in doing the same things and competing with each other on the same stuff. We were very lucky: the boys did the story, Dana did the women and Bruce did the Bond.

CHAPTER THREE

THE STORY

BILBAO, SPAIN

In a private Swiss bank, opposite the famed Guggenheim Museum, a girl wheels a trolley containing cigars into a penthouse office. She hands James Bond (Pierce Brosnan) a briefcase containing £5 million in cash. Bond, acting on M's orders, is retrieving the money on behalf of Sir Robert King, a construction millionaire who is spending the money to buy a classified Russian Atomic Agency report. This had been stolen from an MI6 agent who had been killed in the process. Bond asks the Swiss banker who did it. The banker, surrounded by henchmen, has no intention of saying until Bond flicks a switch on his glasses. There's a flash, a fight in which the henchmen are swiftly dealt with, and Bond holds a gun to the banker's cheek. The man is about to reveal the name of the agent's murderer when a knife hits him in the neck and kills him.

Bond looks up. It was the Cigar Girl (Maria Grazia Cucinotta). She's making her getaway on a wire across the rooftops. A henchmen is killed by a marksman's bullet, another is regaining consciousness, Spanish police are noisily hammering on the door. Bond grabs the cash and a cigar, takes hold of a sash from the window and, using a dazed henchman as ballast, leaps from the window down to the crowded street below.

MI6 HEADQUARTERS, LONDON

Bond, having deposited the money with MI6 Security and the cigar with Miss Moneypenny (Samantha Bond) – 'I know exactly where to put it' – who has duly deposited it in the wastebasket, is thanked for his work by Sir Robert King. They are in M's office. It transpires that Sir Robert is an old friend of M (Judi Dench), having been at Oxford with her. As King leaves to collect his money Bond drops a couple of cubes of ice

into his Talisker whisky and studies the stolen report with the Cyrillic letters 'AEA' on it. He is pondering why they let him get away alive when he notices a strange fizzing in his ice. He rubs his thumb and forefinger together – there is a sizzling. It must have come off the money in the briefcase. It's a set-up. He rushes after King to tell him to stay away from the money. But it is too late. Sir Robert is already in the Security Room and a hum from the his 'Eye of the Glens' lapel-pin activates the metal strips in the money. There is an enormous explosion, which kills King and blasts a hole in the lower Thames-side tier of MI6.

Bond staggers through the swirling dust and smoke to find a wand of red light pointing at his chest. He dives to avoid the bullet which the Cigar Girl fires at him. She is on a speedboat on the river with a high-powered rifle on the stern. Bond rushes in to Q division, where a prototype jet boat is suspended from the ceiling. He leaps into it, presses a button and shoots out of the MI6 building on to the water.

THE THAMES

Bond, in his Q boat, is in hot pursuit of the Cigar Girl. Exchanging fire, they pass the House of Commons and speed on towards Tower Bridge. This is the most amazing river chase you have ever seen, with Bond's boat short-cutting through a fish market, down streets, through restaurants and even using the Cigar Girl's craft as a ramp to barrel-roll ahead of her. He forces her to the edge of the river by the Millennium Dome, where a balloon race is about to set off. Clearing the way with her gun, the Cigar Girl jumps into a basket and pulls the gas nozzle for take-off. As she rises, Bond uses a slipway to propel his boat into the air, leaps from it and grabs

a rope dangling from the balloon. But police helicoptors surround her. The girl suicidally pulls the flame regulator valve knowing her boss, Renard, will come after her if she is caputured. Bond jumps from the massive fireball, fortunately landing on the Millennium Dome, which breaks his fall but leaves him with an injured collar-bone.

THE BANKS OF LOCH LOMOND, SCOTLAND
Many MI6 executives are present as Sir Robert King's body is laid to rest. Bond, his arm in a sling, catches sight of Sir Robert's beautiful daughter, Elektra (Sophie Marceau).

MI6 REMOTE OPERATIONS CENTRE, THANE
CASTLE, SCOTLAND

In the baronial briefing room, Tanner (Michael Kitchen) explains how the banknotes had been dipped into urea, turning them into a bomb, and how King's lapel-pin had been switched for a copy that contained a radio transmitter used to set the bomb off. Robinson (Colin Salmon) says this must have been done by someone close to King, but their only lead is dead. M is angry – 'We will not be terrorized by cowards who would murder an innocent man and use us as a tool' – and determined to hunt down the perpetrators of this atrocity.

Bond, unfortunately, is off the active list owing to his shoulder injury. He has an appointment with Dr Molly Warmflash (Serena Scott Thomas), who is persuaded to give him a clean bill of health after he demonstrates to her he is certainly fit for active service.

Q (Desmond Llewelyn) is less satisfied with him. He had been preparing the craft Bond borrowed – and smashed up – as a fishing boat for his retirement. Q introduces Bond to his new deputy (John Cleese) who demonstrates the latest missile-carrying BMW with big beverage cup holders and also a jerkin which, on the pull of a tag, will balloon up into a huge airbag.

Bond searches the MI6 computer for the file on Elektra King. He discovers from the classified file on her that only a few years ago she was kidnapped but managed to escape, shooting two of her three captors.

He also finds out that the ransom demanded for her release was $5 million, which was the exact sum returned to Sir Robert King. Someone was sending him a message. But further access to her MI6 file is denied. Only M could have sealed it.

Bond confronts his boss with this fact and M admits she had advised Sir Robert not to pay the ransom. Instead she had sent 009 to kill the kidnapper, Renard, an anarchist who operated in the world's major trouble spots.

Elektra escaped before 009 put a bullet in Renard's head. This is killing off his senses but making him stronger and stronger because he has no pain barrier. M orders Bond to go to protect Elektra, who has taken over the construction of her father's pipeline in the Caspian Sea, and find out who snatched the pin.

PIPELINE CONSTRUCTION SITE, CAUCASUS MOUNTAINS, TURKEY

Bond arrives to find the locals in uproar. They are arguing with Davidov (Ulrich Thomsen), King's Chief of Security. They don't want a pipeline built through their village. Elektra King and her hefty bodyguard, Gabor (John Seru), arrive by helicopter. Elektra speaks to the priest in the Coptic church and emerges to tell her men to build the pipeline around the village. The foreman points out that this will cost millions and that her father had approved the route. 'Then my father was wrong,' pronounces Elektra. It is clear who is in charge now.

Elektra recognizes Bond from her father's funeral. He acknowledges that M sent him because they feared her life was in danger. Elektra laughs scornfully. In the office she shows Bond the map of the 800-mile pipeline she is building through Turkey, past the terrorists in Iraq, Iran and Syria. She indicates the Russians' three competing pipelines to the north and says they will do anything to stop her.

Bond tells her they suspect her father's murder might have been the work of an insider and shows her the duplicate lapel-pin with the radio transmitter that caused his death. This stops her cold. 'My family has relied on MI6 twice, Mr Bond, I won't make that mistake a third time.' Nevertheless, Bond is determined to stick with her as she checks the survey lines.

SNOW-CLAD MOUNTAIN TOP

Elektra and Bond hover in a helicopter. The wind is buffeting and the pilot cannot land, so Elektra jumps from the open door and Bond follows. He admires her fearless skiing. They get to the edge of a cliff and Elektra points to the line of survey flags running through the middle of the valley below. 'When the Persian Gulf and all the other oilfields have dried up,' Elektra pronounces, 'this will once again be the heart of the Earth and this pipeline will be the main artery.' They look up and see four dark parahawks coming through towards them, their black canopies spread out like angels of death.

They hear a loud hum, and looking up, see four dark objects. As they plummet towards earth, black canopies spread out slowing their fall and turning them into angels of death.

Bond tells Elektra: 'Head for the gully, I'll lure them to the trees.' She obeys and he slaloms through the woods as the deadly parahawks track him, firing bullets and hurling hand-grenades. One parahawk hits a tree and blows up, but another two are hard on Bond's heels, their bombs exploding in the snow around him. They deftly land and eject their canopies to become snowmobiles. Bond is now caught in an elaborate game of cat and mouse with the three pursuers. Hitting a ski bank, Bond leaps over one as the pilot opens fire but fails to avoid the large pine tree in front of him, crashing into it with another huge explosion. He plays the remaining two off against each other, dramatically putting them on a fatal collision course. Elektra comes alongside Bond on the slope below and he cradles her, protecting her as the two vehicles explode into each other.

They are destined to be buried under tons of snow. This looks like the end but, thank Q, Bond pulls the toggle on his jacket and his airbag opens. It engulfs them as they hit the ground. Elektra is on the verge of hysteria, convinced they are buried alive. Bond holds her tight and asks her to trust him. Everything will be all right. He punches through the snow into the fresh air – and it is.

BEDROOM OF ELEKTRA'S VILLA, BAKU
Through the window, the sun is setting on the Caspian Sea. Elektra asks Bond to tell her who is trying to kill her. He says he doesn't know but will find out. She tells him: 'After the kidnapping I was afraid: afraid to go outside, afraid to be alone, afraid to be in a crowd, afraid to do anything at all until I realized, I can't hide in the shadows. I can't let fear run my life. I won't.' Bond joins her at the window,

saying: 'After I find him, you won't have to.' She caresses his cheek
and pleads with him to stay. But he has his duty to do.

CASINO L'OR NOIR (BLACK GOLD), BAKU
(A GOLDRUSH TOWN IN THE STYLE OF THE
WILD WEST)

Bond, in evening dress, observes the throng through the special
glasses that Q has given him. These enable him to see through
people's clothes. Nearly everyone is armed, and even the girls
have small pistols in their bras. A thug at the bar has a hidden arsenal
– guns, knives, a cudgel. Bond stands next to him and says that

he wants to see Valentin Zukovsky. 'Impossible,' the thug retorts. Bond orders a vodka-martini and says to him: 'Tell him James Bond is here.' The man goes for his gun, but Bond is too quick for him and in a split second the thug is hanging by his tie from the bar.

Bond is led in to see his heavily built friend Zukovsky, once of the Moscow mafia but now the owner of a casino and a caviar factory in Baku. Bond shows him the torn shred of parachute. Zukovsky identifies it as being from the Russian Special Services' Atomic Energy Anti-Terrorist Unit. Bond asks Zukovsky who Renard is working for. Zukovsky is unsure: 'There are four competing pipelines. Half the people in this casino would be happy to see the King pipeline disappear.'

On cue, Elektra arrives, looking impossibly glamorous. Zukovsky offers her her father's chair at the blackjack table and a $1-million line of credit, which she coolly signs for. Bond tries to dissuade her from playing but Elektra retorts: 'There's no point in living if you can't feel alive.' They play one hand. She loses the entire million dollars and gets a buzz of adrenalin from the experience.

FIELD OF FIRE

At this place of Hindu pilgrimage, Renard picks up a scalding rock, as pilgrims used to do. As he watches it sizzling in his hand, he shows no emotion. Davidov has been brought to see him, and Renard asks him how Bond can have seen off four parahawks unarmed. Renard punishes Elektra's security chief by forcing the burning stone into his hand. Arkov, the henchman who deployed the parahawks, has lost his nerve and suggests they abandon their mission. This is the wrong attitude. A nod from Renard and he loses his life. Davidov is given Arkov's ID and told to be on time the next day.

ELEKTRA'S BEDROOM

Afterwards. Elektra tends James's wounded shoulder with some ice. She tells him how she seduced the guards to survive her kidnapping. He leaves her and starts to snoop round the security office at the villa when Davidov arrives

AIRFIELD

Some hours later. Davidov brings his Land Rover to a halt and pulls back the tarpaulin to remove Arkov's dead body. Instead he finds a live Bond with a silenced Walther P99. Bond kills Davidov and takes his place on a departing plane, where he replaces Davidov/Arkov's ID photo with his own.

TEST FACILITY, KAZAKHSTAN

Colonel Akakievich (Claude-Oliver Rudolph) tells 'Dr Arkov' he is a great admirer of his research. Inside a bubble-like protective module a sphere of cobalt-blue plutonium is removed from a corroding warhead. The IDA (International Decommissioning Agency) scientist comes out and takes off her protective suit to reveal a beautiful face and an eye-catching figure in shorts and halter top. Bond introduces himself: 'Mikhail Arkov, Russian Atomic Energy Department.' 'Dr Jones,' says the scientist, 'Christmas Jones. And don't make any jokes. I've heard them all.' 'I don't know any doctor jokes,' Bond replies.

Descending in a elevator into the test chamber, he finds Renard's men working on a nuclear bomb. Bond pulls a gun on Renard, who claims: 'You can't kill me. I'm already dead,' and taunts him with the fact that he had Elektra when she was innocent. Bond is about to kill him but Renard warns him that Elektra will die if he does not make a call. Christmas arrives with the Colonel and two soldiers.

Commander Bond and Dr Jones.

Christmas accuses Bond of being an impostor. He tells her that Renard's men are stealing the bomb. Renard deliberately squeezes Bond's damaged shoulder, causing him to wonder how he knew about the injury.

The Colonel, realizing what is up, tries to stop them removing the bomb without his permission, but it's too late – he and his men are shot by Renard's thugs. Renard gives orders to get the bomb out and seal Bond and Christmas in. But Bond fires the 800lb filament wire from the Omega Seamaster wrist watch that Q gave him and rappels up the side of the pit. He gets a shot at Renard, grazing his arm, but Renard feels no pain. There is a hectic, tense chase on carts, through tunnels, narrowly avoiding closing steel iris doors,

but Renard and his men make it to the elevator with the bomb, leaving a fireball in their wake. Bond retreats in desperation, but Christmas has managed to spark the wires and seal them off from the oncoming wall of fire. They find an elevator that takes them out of the facility and scramble out of a duct into daylight as the whole pit explodes beneath them.

They are just in time to watch Renard's plane take off with the bomb in it, leaving a debris of dead soldiers behind. Christmas tells Bond the terrorists won't get far – they can track the signal of the bomb with its Locator card. Bond removes the card from his breast pocket – 'You mean one of these?'

MI6 REMOTE OPERATIONS CENTRE, THANE CASTLE, SCOTLAND

M and her staff are tracking Renard's plane. Elektra comes on the video line and tells M that Bond is missing and her head of security has been murdered. She implores M to come out to Baku. M agrees.

ELEKTRA'S VILLA, BAKU

Bond confronts Elektra about her relationship with Renard. Her use of his phrase 'There's no point in living if you can't feel alive' and the fact that he knew of Bond's shoulder injury indicate that she is still under his spell. Bond suggests this was a case of the Stockholm Syndrome, in which the captive falls in love with the captor. Elektra denies this, countering that Bond had been using her as bait. The phone rings. Renard has struck again – five men are dead at the pipeline.

PIPELINE CONTROL CENTRE, TURKEY

The room is full of monitors and a huge satellite map of the pipeline. Bond explains why they cannot track the bomb, handing the Locator card to M. He tells her she shouldn't be there. M says he is the reason she is since he disobeyed a direct order and left Elektra alone. Bond suggests that Elektra may have switched the lapel-pin that killed her own father. M is incredulous. But from the map they learn that the bomb is in the pipeline. Is Renard going to blow up the one pipeline that will supply the West with its oil reserves in the next century? Bond asks Christmas: 'What do I need to defuse a nuclear bomb?' She replies: 'Me.'

M loses her cool with Elektra.

INSIDE THE PIPELINE

As if on an insane thrill ride in a theme park, Bond and Christmas hurtle along at 70mph on a rig to catch up with the rig carrying the bomb. They whoosh round a bend and make contact with it.

Bond boards the rig and Christmas follows, attempting in this impossible roller-coaster ride to prise out the plutonium core. She discovers that half the expected plutonium is missing. This indicates that it was not intended to produce a nuclear explosion, and Bond instructs her to let the device blow. They make for the exit hatch in their rig and leap out – just in time. KABOOM! – a section of the pipeline explodes.

PIPELINE CONTROL CENTRE, TURKEY

Gabor reports that the bomb was a dud, but the triggering charge blew out a 50-yard section of pipe. It looks as if Bond and Christmas are dead. Elektra tells M she is sorry and gives her a present – her father's original lapel-pin. Ironically thanking M for the 'compassionate' advice she gave him during the kidnapping, Elektra explains: 'I just couldn't let it explode with the rest of him.' M is horrified by this woman who killed her own father. Gabor shoots M's bodyguard in the head. Elektra tells M: 'I was terribly upset when the bomb didn't kill both of you. I didn't think I'd get another chance.' Elektra's men surround M.

SMOULDERING BROKEN PIPELINE

Bond explains to Christmas that Elektra blew up her own pipeline to make it look like a terrorist attack, to make herself look more innocent and to cover up the theft of the plutonium. They still have half the stolen amount, but it is not enough to make a nuclear bomb. So what are they going to do with it? Bond gets a call to say M is missing with

Elektra. He desperately needs to put the puzzle together. One man can help them – Zukovsky. Next stop, Zukovsky's caviar factory.

MAIDEN'S TOWER, ISTANBUL

The ancient tower at the entrance to the Bosporus. Renard arrives with a present for Elektra – the plutonium. She tells him she has a present for him and leads him to the barred cell where M is imprisoned.

Elektra tells M that MI6 will leave her there to rot, just as M and her father did to her. Renard takes a small travel clock from the shelf and puts it in front of the bars of M's cell, just out of her reach. She, along with Istanbul and 'the bright, starry, oil-driven future of the West', will die at noon tomorrow.

Back in Elektra's bedroom, she and Renard attempt to rekindle their sexual relationship. At first Renard can feel nothing. Then Elektra entices him with an ice cube.

CITY OF WALKWAYS, BAKU

Zukovsky climbs out of his chauffeured Rolls-Royce at his caviar factory, set amid this surreal world of miles of multi-layered wooden walkways linking oil rigs. His chauffeur, nicknamed The Bull (Goldie), remains in the car, spots Bond's BMW and telephones Elektra to tell her that Bond is alive and where he is. Bond and Christmas are waiting for Zukovsky in his office. Bond slams Zukovsky against a vat of caviar. He wants to know what his business is with Elektra – clearly the $1 million which she dropped at the casino was to pay for something.

But the interrogation is interrupted as a giant saw, vertically suspended from a helicopter, rips through the roof. It is normally used to sever branches from massive trees, but this time the pilot is intent on cutting up buildings, walkways and humans. A second chopper appears, the men inside hurling down grenades. Zukovsky's men return fire. Bond darts among the mayhem and hurls himself up a stairway to where he can summon his BMW by remote control. The car comes to life and drives towards him. He jumps in and activates the missile device. But as he lets off a missile and scores a direct hit on the first helicopter, the huge blades of the second slice his car lengthwise. 'You'll answer to Q for that,' Bond observes as he escapes unharmed.

The second chopper drops four armed men. They kill Zukovsky's guards but are no match for Bond, who, in a singular piece of resourcefulness, moves deftly through the walkways and picks them off one by one. As the helicopter bears down on him, he cranks open a gas jet and fires a flare gun into it, causing it to ignite in a fireball.

A free-flying saw blade from the chopper speeds towards Zukovsky, who dives into a caviar pit for safety. As he slowly sinks into the expensive black roe, Bond resumes his interrogation, pointing out that Elektra's blades were meant for Zukovsky as well. But the heavy man is reluctant to talk – until he realizes that without Bond's help he will drown in his own caviar. Yes, he sometimes buys Russian machinery for Elektra, he admits. This time his nephew, Nikoli, who is in the navy, is smuggling some into Istanbul for her.

MAIDEN'S TOWER

Dawn. At the quay, Renard tells Captain Nikoli they are ready to load the cargo into his submarine. Up above, at M's cell, Elektra arrives to bid farewell. M asks her what time it is. Elektra hands her the clock. 'Time for you to die.' When she has gone, M take out the missing Locator card and removes the batteries from the clock to activate it and send out her position.

AN OLD POWER STATION, ISTANBUL

The power station is full of Soviet generators and staff who are operating spying equipment as if the Cold War had never ended. There is a large map of the Bosporus Strait and the Black Sea. When Zukovsky casually reveals that they are looking for his nephew's 'submarine', Bond immediately gets the picture. They want to use the reactor. Christmas spells it out: 'Put weapons-grade plutonium in that sub's reactor – instant, catastrophic meltdown.' Bond explains Elektra's master plan: she is orchestrating an explosion – made to look like an accident – that would destroy Istanbul and contaminate the Bosporus for decades. The tankers from the existing northern pipelines would no longer be able to use the port and the only way to get oil out would be through the King pipeline to the south.

A radio operator is getting a signal. Bond realizes it is from the Locator card he gave to M. They run the co-ordinates against the map. She is in the Maiden's Tower. As they discover this, The Bull puts a briefcase on a chair and scoots out of the door. Bond spots him and grabs Christmas. 'Bomb!' He manages to pull her behind a generator to shelter from the blast.

Bond and Christmas race after The Bull, out of the power station and round the corner, straight into a planned trap – Gabor and his men. It's no contest. The Bull removes Bond's gun as he and Christmas are taken to the Maiden's Tower.

SUBMARINE

Nikoli and his crew are dead – poisoned. Renard takes Nikoli's hat as a souvenir. On the quay Renard confirms to Elektra that the reactor is secured. Her helicopter will arrive in half an hour. 'This is end,' he says. Elektra corrects him: 'No. This is the beginning. The world will never be the same.' Renard gives her the captain's hat as a farewell present.

MAIDEN'S TOWER

Elektra orders Christmas to be taken away to the submarine. She has other plans for Bond, leading him to an ornate room with an exotic view of Istanbul. Gabor and a fellow thug bind him to an upright chair, handsomely carved and covered in silk. 'I could have given you the world,' she tells him. He looks at her. 'The world is not enough.' She goes over to his chair, telling him how it had been found in an historical dig. Reaching behind his neck, she flips out a metal collar which whips round his neck – a garrotte. 'Five more turns and your neck will break,' she informs him as she makes the first turn of the screw.

This is no longer the innocent, frightened young woman he had come to protect. Her bitterness at men had been reinforced by her father's refusal to pay the ransom. When he wouldn't rescue her she had to form a new alliance – with her kidnappers. Bond gets it: 'You turned Renard.' Elektra turns the screw again, her eyes blazing with her megalomania. 'It's my oil. It runs in my veins, thicker than blood.

I'm going to redraw the map. And when I am through the whole world will know my name, my grandfather's name, the glory of my people.'

Bond's response that nobody will buy the 'accident' is met with Elektra's amazement that he has worked out her plan and a further tightening of the screw. She straddles him, cruelly enquiring: 'Know what happens when a man is strangled?' Bond implores her to spare the lives of eight million people. A penultimate turn of the screw. She looks at him scornfully. 'You should have killed me when you had the chance. But you couldn't. Not me. A woman you've loved.'

As her hand goes to the bolt, Bond stutters: 'One ... last ... screw?' Could this be his epitaph? Not yet. Gunshots outside. Zukovsky and his men are fighting their way into the building. Elektra moves to her gun. Gabor is killed. Zukovsky bursts into the room. 'I'm looking for a submarine. It's big and black and the driver is a friend of mine.'

Then he sees Nikoli's hat and realizes what must have happened. 'Bring it to me,' he demands. Elektra turns and does so, but slips a gun under the hat and releases three bullets into Zukovsky's chest.

As the giant slumps to the floor, close to death, he summons up his last ounce of strength to aim the gun at Bond. Elektra is amused that this will now be 007's death. Blam! The shot goes off but it misses.

Elektra fails to notice that Zukovsky's aim was perfect – he hit the binding on Bond's wrist. Neither does she notice the merest exchange of smiles between the two men.

She picks up her walkie-talkie to tell Renard that everything is under control. He bids her au revoir. Returning her attention to Bond, she plants a kiss on his lips and herself on his lap as she reaches to twist the screw one last, fateful time. But Bond's hand breaks free, grabs her throat and throws her on to the floor.

On his feet again, he picks up the gun. Elektra is fast disappearing upstairs. He grabs the walkie-talkie and follows her.

Elektra is running up one of the triple spiral stairways leading to the balconies of the minaret tower. Her voice echoes downwards: 'James. You can't kill me. Not in cold blood.'

Another voice comes from the semi-darkness. 'Bond!' It is M in her cell. Instinctively he fires a shot, breaking the massive lock on her door.

But he has his own agenda. He catches up with Elektra and hands her the walkie-talkie: 'Call him off.' Elektra taunts him: 'You wouldn't kill me – you'd miss me.' Then she screams into the mouthpiece: 'Renard! Dive. Bond ...'

And that is her last word. The bullet has gone neatly through her heart. 'I never miss,' says 007. Behind him, M has seen it all.

From the balcony of the tower he can see the submarine moving out into the Bosporus. He composes himself, dives the hundred feet into the water, grabs a ladder leading up on to the sub, hits the amazed sailor who is closing the hatch with the hatch itself and slips into the vessel milliseconds before it slides under the water.

THE SUBMARINE – UNDER THE BOSPORUS

Bond approaches a crewman, holds his gun to his head and demands to know where Christmas is. He finds her and she is amazed to see him. They move through the shadows to the window of the submarine's control room. Bond gun-butts the buoyancy control crewman and, covering the rest of the crew with his gun, pulls down the two emergency handles which operate the aft buoyancy tanks.

Alarms sound. A loud hiss of air. Renard rushes in with his gun. He and Bond exchange shots but the submarine has begun to tilt alarmingly.

Fire from the crew haphazardly shatters the control panels, so they are unable to fulfil Renard's order to get the sub level. It lunges through ninety degrees and now hangs vertically, nose down.

As the crewmen lose their grip and fall, the helmsman accidentally hits the engine control, setting it to 'Full Ahead'. Bond and Christmas grab hold of the cargo netting as the sub rams nose first into the bed of the Bosporus.

Bond and Christmas struggle into the control room, which is filling up with water. Christmas sees a panel light up. 'He's opened the reactor and locked himself in,' she warns. 'And us out,' says Bond. Then he spots the escape chamber. 'There's one chance.'

Using the escape hatch, Bond makes his way up the outside of the submarine, past the horizontal conning tower, to the rear hatch.

He looks down into the reactor room bathed in the horrible light of the overheating reactor. Renard's back is to him. Bond swings down, hitting Renard in the back with both feet and smashing him headlong into the reactor.

The water in the control room has now brought Christmas, still breathing, up to the lower door. Bond jumps down and pulls her in. She points to the slowly bubbling reactor core, and says: 'We're safe from the radiation as long as the reactor coolant doesn't burst. If he had got the plutonium in the reactor, you could have written off the whole city.'

A fist sends Bond sprawling. He spots the plutonium bar on the floor, just out of his reach. 'You're really going to commit suicide for her?' he asks Renard. 'In case you've forgotten,' the terrorist replies, 'I'm dead already.' Bond regards him callously. 'Haven't you heard the news? So is she.'

For the first time we see real pain on Renard's face. 'You're lying,' he screams, but he knows he isn't. Bond grabs the plutonium bar and hits the side of Renard's head. But it only momentarily stuns him. Renard smashes Bond against the steel-mesh floor, forcing him to drop the bar. The catch fastening the mesh opens and Bond falls through. Renard pulls the mesh closed again and secures it.

Bond has to watch in agonized frustration as Renard slowly inserts the plutonium rod. As the temperature rises towards the fatal 5000 degrees, Bond catches sight of the central coupling at the end of the core. It is used for flushing and cleaning the control rod chambers. He grabs a thrashing hose pipe and attaches it to the coupling. Then he watches the pressure gauge. Yes! It's building. But so is the temperature gauge. Nearly 5000. It's neck and neck. Which will blow first?

WHOOMF!!!

The built-up pressure of the steam blows the plutonium rod back out of the reactor and impales Renard through the heart. He stares at Bond in horror. 'She's waiting for you,' 007 tells him impassively.

Christmas unbolts the steel mesh to let Bond out and reinserts the control rods in the reactor. She wants to get out of there but Bond points to the gauge on the wall. 'The hydrogen gas level is too high. One spark and the whole thing will blow. We'll have to flood it.'

Christmas climbs ahead to the mine room. Bond opens the control room hatch and floods the reactor room. He floats up with the encroaching water, sets a timer to 'Fire' and follows Christmas into the Mine Launching Tube.

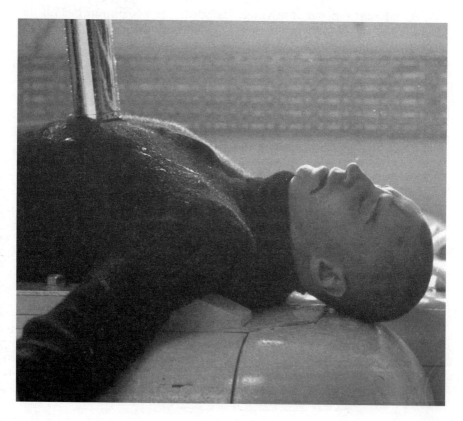

Extreme skier.

Avalanche alert.

Explosion: nuclear facility.

Explosion: walkways.

Leaving Maiden's Tower.

A swim in the Bosporus.

Oil walkways on Pinewood's Paddock Tank.

Elektra's ski suit.

Gun.

Nuclear device.

MI6 exterior design

MI6 interior design.

BMW

The launching doors open and Bond and Christmas are shot out into the water just as the submarine explodes. They reach the surface. Their luck is still in – a tourist boat diverts to pick them up. Better than the Titanic.

RESTORED MI6 BRIEFING ROOM, LONDON
M and her staff are scrutinizing a satellite thermal image of Istanbul. It zooms in on Bond. 'Where is he?' M demands. R explains that the thermal image picks up body heat. 'Humans should be orange.' They see just one orange figure on a balcony. 'I thought you said he was with Dr Jones?' says Tanner. The orange figure begins to turn redder and redder. M and Tanner realize at the same time that this is an image of two people, one on top of the other and getting hotter. Miss Moneypenny averts her gaze from the screen. 'Could be a premature form of the Millennium Bug,' R remarks.

BALCONY, ISTANBUL
A balmy night, twinkling stars, the soft moans of seagulls. A couple are entwined on a sunbed. 'I suppose I was wrong about you,' Bond concedes. 'How so?' asks Dr Jones. 007 smiles. 'I thought Christmas only comes once a year'.

CHAPTER FOUR

BOND'S GIRLS

Six actresses feature in *The World Is Not Enough*, their ages ranging from 27 to 64: Sophie Marceau, Judi Dench, Denise Richards, Samantha Bond, Serena Scott Thomas and Maria Grazia Cucinotta.

In a film series that has as its intent nothing other than undiluted escapist entertainment, the only aspect of the real world that can sometimes cause problems is the positioning of the Bond girls in terms of political correctness.

No one had thought of placing the words 'politically' and 'correct' together when Ursula Andress emerged from the sea in *Dr No* in 1962. With her knife tucked in her bikini, Honey Ryder wasn't just part of the Swinging Sixties – she was an icon of the era: a woman who was bright, beautiful, self-determined and downright dangerous. Others who followed in her footsteps had to live up or down to their names, which did not always hit the heights of subtlety: Pussy Galore, Plenty O'Toole, Mary Goodnight and Dr Holly Goodhead. By the time of the Dalton Bonds such fun and puns were firmly set aside – Carey Lowell even carried the maiden name of Mrs Kennedy Onassis in Pam 'Bouvier'.

With the Brosnan Bonds some brave soul put his toe in the water again and named a character Xenia Onatopp and, amazingly, the world continued to revolve and no riots or stampedes broke out. Perhaps feminists thought Bond was beyond the pale – or didn't think about him at all.

But the subject is still a touch-paper waiting to be ignited, as Michael Apted found to his cost when he spoke to a newspaper reporter. He tells the story with the relative safety of hindsight:

I was doing a seminar on my films, particularly my documentaries, at the Sheffield Film Festival and the Festival rang me and asked if the

Daily Telegraph could do an interview. I said yes and a nice girl rang me up on Sunday morning and we talked about documentaries. She asked if I could say anything about the Bond film and I said fine and she asked some question to which I replied that women were at the heart of the film and I wanted to make the women more interesting. We probably spoke for three minutes out of the 30-minute interview on that. The following day I was on the plane to Istanbul to scout locations and someone said to me, 'You'd better take a look at this.' Half of page three of the *Daily Telegraph* was filled with pictures of former Bond girls accompanied by a piece about how I was going to rewrite the law about Bond women. 'No More Bikinis,' it said. Forget bikinis, women have now got to be brainy and all that sort of stuff. Then the popular press picked it up and they slagged me off. They called me a boring, grey-haired, liberal intellectual who is going to wreck Bond. It was all very jolly. But the studio got extremely jumpy about it and asked me what on earth I was doing. It was pretty tricky because I'd put my foot in it.

In fact, the current film has a greater variety of women than ever before. Bond conducts romantic entanglements with 50 per cent of the six featured females in the film and one of them is even called Dr Molly Warmflash.

ELEKTRA KING is the pivotal female part in *The World Is Not Enough* – not only a more enigmatic woman than Bond has ever encountered before but, deep down, a character as fanatical as Dr No, Ernst Blofeld and Auric Goldfinger combined. It was said that the studio saw Sharon Stone in the part since she had clocked up quite a few miles as latter-day Lady Macbeths. But the Bond production team thought that this would be too obvious casting. The whole point about Elektra was that Bond – and the audience – should fall under her spell at first sight.

Apted was very keen on SOPHIE MARCEAU, the French actress who stepped on to a broader world stage when Mel Gibson cast her in *Braveheart* (she later played leads in English in *Firelight* and *Anna Karenina*). 'I really fought for her,' the director says:

As soon as I met her, I knew she was the real thing for this. She was absolutely intoxicating to look at and because the trick of the film is that you can't believe she's the villain even if the publicity tells you, when you first see her, you think: this can't be true. Of all the women I saw for the role, you immediately fell in love with this woman, which I thought was crucial. We have to go through the same process. There had to be a short-hand. You couldn't spend ten minutes of the film with her and Bond falling in love. You had to know that as soon as he saw her he was in some sort of trouble. The more I talked to Sophie the more I realized she did have the range to pull off the huge arc that the character takes – unbelievable. At the beginning you have to be in love with her and at the end you have to be happy that he kills her. You have to think: she deserved that.

Sophie Marceau recalls that when she was invited to read the 'garrotte' scene for Michael Wilson, Apted and the casting director, Debbie McWilliams. 'It's where I sit him in an old garrotte chair,' she smiles. 'It's a seduction and an au revoir in a dramatic way.' They then invited her to screen-test and this focused again on this same scene which reveals the iniquitous paradox of Elektra's character: that she is prepared to torture a man to death, while using him for her pleasure.

Sophie was intrigued to be the villain in a Bond film. She explained:

You don't have to play the villain, because the villain doesn't think she's a villain. She thinks she's defending a cause. A Bond film is a fantasy, some-thing that is totally abstract in a way. I don't have to be conscious about being the villain because the film is conscious about it. It's a big relief when the actor doesn't have to tell the story but just be the character.

At the same time, even though a Bond film may be fantasy, you have to build up a character who is as credible as possible. She's a tough girl. We see at the beginning that she disregards her father's wishes and puts the pipeline round the village – she cares about the villagers and the village. She has power, she leads a big company, she is immensely rich, she comes from two cultures – Turkish and English (plus mine – French). She's a mixture of different contradictions which make her background a very interesting case. She could be a cliché but then there is this trauma that happened in the past – the kidnapping – that changed the whole face of the character.

As an actress I just think about the story between people, the relationship between her and M, Bond and her, coupled with the Renard affair, which was something difficult to define and make clear. I think through the subtlety of the relationships you can draw a profile of a character going through the film. The consequences of her actions are the explosions and things – all the entertaining stuff, but the film does that.

Sophie grew up in the French countryside. There were not many cinemas nearby, so film did not play a big part in her life. 'I went with my mother once or twice to see Roger Moore as Bond. He was very popular when I was 15. And it's the young generation in Paris today – people of 18 or 20 – who know and tell me, "Great that you're making a Bond film."'

She has found working in English something of an education:

I once went to drama school but it was not for me. For me acting was just acting. Thirteen films is the best training. It is sometimes hard to distance yourself and analyse what acting is. It's an interesting thing, it evolves. There are so many possibilities in this film being directed by an English director. English is a language for performance, for being acted. It's very precise and sharp and short and each word intonation has a meaning. Everything is on the same level, so a tiny difference could just change the whole thing and give more emotion than probably if you were to show it. So it's a good school. I think it will help my acting in French.

DR CHRISTMAS JONES is an altogether different kettle of fish. Few of us meet nuclear scientists from the International Decommissioning Agency in day-to-day life. The cliché is that they are rumpled boffins, so how refreshing to meet someone as clear-eyed and limber as the character played by DENISE RICHARDS, her string of degrees as fresh as her complexion.

Apted is candid about her casting:

I knew with Christmas that I wanted to walk the tightrope between delivering a sexy Bond girl and to try and get something more out of her. I had had a shock with the press stuff. Denise seemed to us to be a very obvious choice. She's very hot – she's a young 'comer'. There's a lot of attention around her. Again I tested quite a few women but clearly she was the one who was right to do it. She looked great. She was clearly interested in acting and didn't just want to be decoration, and had a great interest in the character and bringing it alive.

Some indication of Denise's burgeoning popularity is her status as an Internet darling. She has more websites than a forest of spiders. You can surf her life: Born on 17 February 1972, Downers Grove, Illinois, USA. High School: El Camino, Oceanside, California. Graduated 1989. Modelling assignments in New York, Paris and Japan. Switched to acting and appeared in several television series including *Melrose Place*. After feature film debut in *Loaded Weapon 1* (1993) she broke through as the gutsy pilot Carmen Ibanez in Paul Verhoeven's *Starship Troopers* (where she met her boyfriend Patrick Muldoon), she stole the screen in *Wild Things* (playing opposite Kevin Bacon) with her now infamous threesome scene and in July 1999 she starred with Kirstie Alley in *Drop Dead Gorgeous*, a satirical send-up of the world of beauty queens. 'This lady is headed somewhere!' says the www. Height: five feet six inches.

Certainly Denise's highest-profile job to date is as Dr Christmas Jones. She explains her take on the role: 'I talked the character through with Michael Apted. But every actor has to bring something of their own to the part. Christmas is very smart. There's a lot of spunk to her. She likes danger; in fact, she's fearless. And she plays well off of Bond. They spark each other. There's a nice contrast between my character and Sophie's.'

It's an all-action part – she has to accompany Bond on a series of escapades, from the fight in the nuclear facility to the chase through the pipeline to defuse the nuclear bomb to the nightmare night on the oilfield walkways to the death submarine. Denise likes action. 'I think it's fun and it helps with the dialogue if you have something to do. Michael Apted has a personal vision of certain scenes. It's necessary to take Bond seriously, but you add to that a little tongue-in-cheek humour.'

A particular challenge came in some of the action scenes. 'I'd ask Pierce for his advice quite a lot. This is his third Bond, so he's done a lot of action. He'd show me the easiest way to fall or suggest when I should put pads on. And then, of course, if it got too risky we'd have doubles.'

Denise won the admiration of Simon Crane, the stunt co-ordinator, who pronounced:

She's got a great attitude. In the final submarine sequence she has to do a lot of underwater shots. She'd never done it before, but she was really keen to learn. She started off on the side of the tank where it was very shallow and just ducked her head under at first. All the stunt men are diving instructors, so she's been on a crash diving course. And also she had to do something that divers don't do. When she was underwater she had to take all the diving equipment off, do an entire sequence and then grab another piece of air at the end. She did it wonderfully.

DAME JUDI DENCH, in her third incarnation as M, is not required to perform any underwater stunts in the film – her activity tends to be more mental – but she does get captured in the Maiden's Tower in Istanbul. 'I'm in this cell and Pierce shoots the lock off. I haven't been in a scene where guns were used before. It was all very exciting, thrilling.'

She was thrilled by the increase in her part, too, courtesy of Michael Apted. 'I had three days on *GoldenEye*, five on *Tomorrow Never Dies* and 14 on this one. I was going to be in Scotland – which I would have adored – and in Turkey. But the nearest I got was being in a trailer called Innsbruck in Buckinghamshire.'

But Dame Judi relished the more emotional journey that her role was allowed to take:

It was very well written. It seemed to me to be terribly clear that there was an agenda between Sir Robert King and M. They were up at Oxford together reading law. It might not have been a relationship that came to anything but certainly from her point of view he was somebody she had been very attracted to. Sir Robert was played by David Calder, who's an old friend of ours, so that was nice on the first day. And it's because of M's relationship with King, that when she sees Elektra on the screen and she says, 'Please can you come out to me', there's an emotional involvement that makes her do it.

Dame Judi needed little persuading to return to a Bond film. She told me:

I'm a company person and that's why this is lovely because I come back to see lots of people I know and a character I think I kind of know about. Therefore it's not quite so frightening for me. On the first one Pierce and I were both frightened to begin with but Martin Campbell was very calm and very clear. Michael Apted is very much an actors' director — I'd never worked with him before but I just knew straight away. He's like John Madden (who directed her in *Mrs Brown* and *Shakespeare In Love*). They give you a bit of breathing space and a bit of leeway to do something within their framework. It's a great luxury. I still can never bring myself to look at rushes. It's too late for you to amend something and that is just very frustrating for me.

How about video playback?

'No. I couldn't watch that either. I have a different vision of myself than I see.'

In what way?

'I'm a tall, willowy person,' she added with a laugh.

This time Dame Judi came to the part better prepared than ever before. She had actually been to lunch at MI6 – a rare entry into a closed world. All the big chiefs are known by letters – M, in real life, is actually called C and does write all his memoranda in green ink as has been rumoured. The secret agents told Judi that they all watched the Bond films but preferred the bits with girls to the bits with the gadgets as they've seen those before. I asked her if there was anyone like Q in the building. 'Many,' was the wicked reply.

Dame Judi's eminence in America now causes people to write to her and ask if she's done anything else except M and *Mrs Brown*. 'You think, there goes 41 years whizzing over your shoulder,' she said resignedly.

We talked in the aforementioned trailer in Buckinghamshire. It was necessary to film all her scenes at the beginning of the film so that she could fulfil a contract to play in *Amy's View* by Sir David Hare on Broadway. Before that she had a night at the Oscars, where she was nominated for her Queen Elizabeth in *Shakespeare In Love*. She told me there was no chance of her winning as she was only on the screen for eight minutes. I'm pleased to say that on my tape of our conversation I advised her to prepare a speech since the Academy voters tend to aggregate the previous year's performance as well. As it transpired, she was the recipient of a much-deserved Oscar.

By a total coincidence SAMANTHA BOND in her third bout as MISS MONEYPENNY, the world's most famous secretary, was also off to Broadway, to play Judi Dench's daughter in Sir Richard Eyre's production of *Amy's View*. The two women have a bitter falling out in the play and Samantha sees their personal friendship as an asset in this respect. 'I think you'd have much more of a problem playing fiction if you didn't get on. I think that the friendship and affection that is genuine between us means that when we are playing the warmth between the mother and the daughter, our private relationship can only strengthen that.'

I asked her how different Moneypenny was from Samantha Bond in speech and appearance. Her reply was immediate: 'She isn't. She looks and sounds just like Samantha Bond.'

And character?

If we were to talk about my approach to acting, it would be picking out the bits within me that are relevant to whoever the 'she' is that one is playing at the time. I'm married with two children. Moneypenny isn't married, doesn't have any children, she's 'lighter' than I am – no maternal worries. So what you kind of do is put the 'heavy' bits of you, the dark bits of you, away, just because they're inappropriate. But when you play a part like Amy, that's when you have to end up with as much weight as a youngish woman can deal with.

She is in a good position to observe Pierce. '*In GoldenEye* he was so outrageously pretty that you kind of think: Oh, don't be silly. Nobody looks like that. But now he's getting that chiselled, slightly older look and I think he's becoming more attractive. He's growing into James and James is growing into him.'

So would Moneypenny ever succumb to his charms? 'She adores him, she gets terribly worried if he gets into trouble and that's a sign of the depth of her affection for him. But I don't think she's pining. It's just a jolly flirt. I don't think for one moment that it would be anything else – unless, of course, he grew up.'

One of the wittiest members of the permanent cast, Samantha acknowledges her part is not enormous. 'My husband and I were having dinner with Barbara Broccoli and she said I'm one of the parts that are a "quick fix" – you need people who can make an impact in 30 seconds because that's all they've got. It's much easier playing parts where you have a through line and the character goes somewhere.'

So where does Moneypenny go when she's not on screen? 'I think she's having a long bath.'

There is a certain symmetry in the part of DR MOLLY WARMFLASH being the first Bond role for actress SERENA SCOTT THOMAS. Her very first feature film was *Let Him Have It* (1991) from the pen of the Bond writers Neal Purvis and Robert Wade. Educated at Cheltenham Ladies' College, like her elder sister Kristin Scott Thomas (internationally known for *The English Patient*), Serena is not afraid to shock and managed to upset a few old school friends by playing Diana, Princess of Wales in the TV mini-series based on Andrew Morton's book *Diana: Her True Story*. In the current Bond film she may shock the medical profession by her violation of the Hippocratic oath when she gives 007 a clean bill of health in exchange for some very unprofessional services.

Serena is now married to a Californian lawyer and regards flying home to England for three days of filming with James Bond as 'one of the more enjoyable aspects of being an actress. I get to do a bit of canoodling and give an elaborate medical explanation of the medulla oblongata. I think being in a Bond film is something every actress should do – if she gets the chance. Pierce Brosnan is a sweetie – really fun, he doesn't have any of that ridiculous macho thing. He's normal, which maybe you shouldn't be being James Bond.'

The words Dr Warmflash are never actually mentioned during the film: Bond calls her Molly and M wryly notes: 'I see the good doctor has cleared you. Notes you have "exceptional stamina."'

The CIGAR GIRL is the Woman with No Name, as she is referred to as 'Cigar Girl' in the credits and without nomenclature in the movie. However, few who saw her as Beatrice opposite Massimo Troisi in *Il Postino* (1995) will forget the dark charms of MARIA GRAZIA CUCINOTTA.

'She's a killer,' she says of her part:

She is just a soldier and Renard is the general. I jumped at the chance to work with Robert Carlyle – I love all his movies. He's a great actor – short, but great. In Bilbao I had to jump from a window – I just did the first metre. The streets were carpeted with people – I couldn't see the ground. With this film, you know you're doing something popular. It's already very big in Italy. After *Il Postino* I did another 15 movies but when they got the news I was doing this I got all the magazine covers and newspapers and television – it was like I had won an Oscar. It was uncanny, but I appreciated that.

Much of Maria's work is a chase on the River Thames. 'I'm doing all the fun here with a boat on the river. It's very exciting. I want to do everything myself. I drive the boat. I grew up in Sicily and I know how to drive a boat. This one is better than a car. Only when I have to jump do they use the double.'

She doesn't seem to mind the fact her character has no name. 'So she doesn't have a name. Maybe she has a number.'

CHAPTER FIVE

SCOTTISH SCOUNDRELS

There was a time – during the first decade of the Bond series –
when the hero of the films was a Scotsman. Sean Connery, once
an Edinburgh milkman and coffin polisher, broke into show business
through the Mr Universe competition and the chorus of *South Pacific*
and became the first movie 007 in *Dr No* in 1962. Ian Fleming may
have written the character in his own image – Eton and the Royal
Navy – but it was a 30-year-old Scot of humbler origins that
undoubtedly gave Bond mass screen appeal.

Nowadays, however, that devolved country, with its new parliament
and revitalized identity, is providing Bond villains rather than heroes.
Robbie Coltrane as Valentin Zukovsky in *GoldenEye* was on the wrong
side of the law – he ran the mafia in St Petersburg – but has come round to
the right side of Bond, after being his adversary in an earlier Cold War
incarnation. He still limped, thanks to a bullet in the leg from 007, but the
two became blood brothers in pursuit of a common enemy.

Zukovsky returns in *The World Is Not Enough*, still a scoundrel but more
007-friendly than ever before. However, the architect of all evil in the
movie is RENARD, played by another Scot, ROBERT CARLYLE, who
found worldwide fame as the irresistible star of *The Full Monty*.

Carlyle grew up in Glasgow and in awe of Sean Connery:

My father would take me to see those films in the sixties and early seventies, and – this is genuine – I honestly believed he was the only Scottish
actor because he was the only person that, when you went to the movies,
sounded a bit like me. There was a fundamental reason for my being
involved in this whole thing. This guy was at the forefront for so many
years. I have a reputation for playing a lot of villains. The whole thing
seemed to go hand-in-hand, so it was a very easy reason for me to say yes
to the part.

One of the main reasons he was offered the part was that Michael Wilson saw him acting opposite Robbie Coltrane in the television series *Cracker*, in which Coltrane plays a police psychologist. Carlyle appeared in the part of Albie, a man who survived the mayhem that killed so many Liverpool football fans at Sheffield's Hillsborough stadium, but, after reading in the *Sun* newspaper that the supporters were 'scum', took his revenge on the world in a series of psychopathic murders.

Wilson felt that one day Carlyle could be a very powerful Bond villain. When Bobby was cast and started to work on the part, although he didn't know that this was due to his *Cracker* character, his instinct was to shave the mane of hair that made him so appealing in *The Full Monty* and reassert the fearsome skinhead appearance of Albie. 'It was the first time I'd had my hair like that since *Cracker*,' he says. 'And the first day Robbie Coltrane saw me on the Bond set he went: "My God, it's like a flashback." Then I learnt they'd been looking at tapes of *Cracker* and everything seemed to have been written beforehand.'

Carlyle, whippet thin with piercing eyes, has an earnestness of both mind and body. Many people might be surprised that an actor of his intensity would appear in a genre of commercial film that would seem to be slightly off his beaten track. He agrees:

This type of work is entirely different from what I've been involved in. It's a wonderful, wonderful fantasy. It's about look and effect and the fact that from scene one this is the bad guy. There isn't really an awful lot of time to draw these things out from within yourself as the film progresses. So in that respect I changed the whole way that I work, because for me it's always from inside. I had discussions with Michael Apted about it. OK, this guy feels no pain. How far does this go? Is this emotional? If you don't feel physical or emotional pain, then you don't feel anything – you're a complete vacuum, you're nothing. So we had to come and go a little bit with that.

I was intrigued to learn how and where he decided to draw the line. He knew precisely:

Through Elektra. That's really the focus of the whole film for Renard. The only feelings that he has are for this woman. He is prepared to do anything for her. He is still completely obsessed with her. He will die for her. He would die for her even if he wasn't dying already. Working with Sophie has been fantastic. She has been so determined to make a success of this because it's a second language for her. We have this very abortive attempt at a love scene. She tries partly to seduce him but, of course, Renard doesn't feel anything, so there's terrible frustration there and it makes him smash his hand through a table. There's a lot of sexual tension in this film, very very different from the sexual agenda in most of the movies. The women's parts are far more complex and deeper than they've been before.

And depth and complexity are two elements that Carlyle imported into the role of Renard; he wanted to get as far away as possible from the much-parodied type of Bond villain who strokes a white cat or keeps killer fish in an indoor pond. In the script Renard is an alias for Victor Zokas, a Russian anarchist of the eighties. But Carlyle studied more recent world events to create his character.

You have to give yourself some kind of platform, some kind of background and I've taken the conflict in Yugoslavia as the basis for the whole thing. I told an actor friend I was thinking of doing this and he introduced me to a Bosnian actor, Velibor Topic — a fantastic guy. I think he was in Macedonia when it happened big time in Sarajevo, where he lived, and he was cut off from his country. He told me incredible stories and I started to think about someone from a military background in a similar situation being confronted with the horrors of war and seeing the whole mess that had been created in that part of the world was not going to be sorted out quickly – as was proved – and there was the opportunity to make cash the easiest way possible through terrorism and kidnapping. There was no love for Elektra to begin with. She was purely a financial target.

It is Carlyle's contention that Bond villains have come a long way since the sixties and seventies:

Times have changed. There was a fantastic innocence about those films. I think most people who have power or a degree of control have charisma. Someone asked me the other day that if charisma had a colour, what would it be? I said 'pink'. And funnily enough that's what people who are into that kind of stuff say – that charisma is pink. And I think Renard's kind of pink. He has something about him – a certain gait and a certain way which means that people will look at him, people will take time to observe him and I think if you have that, you have charisma.

Of course Pierce Brosnan has it coming out of every pore. A charismatic man and a charismatic actor. I think he's breathed new life into the whole piece. The reality of the situation is that this guy is licensed to kill and you have to be looking at an actor who's capable of communicating that and I think Pierce has got it in his eyes. You believe his Bond could kill you. I think with people like me and Judi Dench on board you can bring the story a little further down the road. It can get a bit more frightening. There's a moment at the end of this film – the final confrontation between Bond and Renard – where Bond tells Renard that Elektra is dead and my reaction is one hundred per cent absolute rage. It looks as if

Renard is going to basically beat him to death. It should look like this is the last Bond movie.

In the course of filming Robert Carlyle was presented with an OBE by the Queen for his services to acting. 'What are you doing at the moment?' the Monarch politely enquired of the actor at the investiture at Buckingham Palace. 'I've spent the week trying to kill James Bond, ma'am,' the thespian honestly replied.

But if he were not to succeed, if Bond were to prevail, will this be Carlyle's only Bond movie? The Scottish actor smiles. 'There's an old actors' superstition in the theatre that if you want to come back you leave your soap in the shower. I'll be leaving my soap in the shower.'

ROBBIE COLTRANE must have done just this at the end of *GoldenEye*. Apart from the home team, he is not the first actor to leave his soap behind. Richard Keil must have done so in *The Spy Who Loved Me* (1977) as his infamous Jaws turned up again in *Moonraker* (1979). Anthony Dawson played Ernst Stavro Blofeld in *From Russia With Love* (1963) and *Thunderball* (1965) – with Donald Pleasence, Telly Savalas and Charles Gray taking over the part in subsequent films. The record for the most shrunk soap must go to David Hedison, who reappeared as Felix Leiter in *Licence To Kill* (1989) after a 16-year break – the American created the part in *Live And Let Die* (1973).

Michael France, the first scriptwriter on *GoldenEye*, who is credited with the story, actually created Zukovsky but Bruce Feirstein changed his character into that of a Sydney Greenstreet. 'If you look at his first appearance at *GoldenEye*,' says Feirstein,' you'll see he's sitting at a table negotiating about weapons when he holds the gun at that guy.'

The first writers on *The World Is Not Enough*, Neal Purvis and Robert Wade, well steeped in Bond lore, knew they had the power to bring back characters. In many ways a familiar face made their job easier. 'It's great knowing who you're writing for,' Wade admits. 'So we had the idea of bringing Zukovsky back and we suggested him having a casino in the Caspian.'

'His having been ex-St Petersburg mafia, it's a natural progression,' Purvis interpolates.

'And we wanted to dump him in a vat of caviar.' Wade smiles with the satisfaction that only a writer can have when he has come up with neat way of hoisting a character with his own petard – and knows he doesn't have to do the dirty work himself.

So it was that Robbie Coltrane – triple British Academy Award winner for *Cracker* – spent two and a half damp January nights from dusk to dawn in a vast vat of caviar on top of the exterior Paddock Tank at Pinewood. Well, not quite caviar. 'They had terrible trouble coming up with something that looked like caviar,' Coltrane recalls. 'I think they ended up with sago pudding that was dyed black in wallpaper paste.'

In the scene Zukovsky dives to save himself from the giant helicopter saw that is chewing up the walkways, and ends up in this heaving pit of caviar. He slowly sinks, as into quicksand, with Bond refusing to help him out until he tells him the truth about Elektra.

'The first night was my birthday,' Coltrane remembers ruefully:

Coltrane in the vat.

We were there all night. It was warm when I got into it and immediately turned ice cold. It was the part of the film I was least looking forward to but like all these things, once you know it's going to be dreadful you prepare yourself and it's much more fun than you think. I had a wet suit on, which goes some way to keeping you warm, but it was pretty miserable. You have to decide whether it's worth getting out between takes and it isn't really. By the time they get you out, hose you down and dry you off, getting back in is so miserable that you're better off staying in. The medical people monitored me the whole time. But it was cold and miserable and I was glad to get off the set in the morning. At the side of the set was a big hot tub and I just threw myself in with all my clothes on. That was lovely.

Coltrane is fascinated by film. After he left Glasgow School of Art he produced and directed a 50-minute documentary, Young Mental Health, which won the Scottish Education Council Film of the Year Award for 1973.

I like films. I'm really into making them. At art school I was interested in directing Super 8 low-budget art films, but now I really like big movies. Proper films. I'm writing a thriller at the moment, which is my favourite genre. I like it on the Bond set, sitting around for two hours and suddenly it's all action. It's like being in the army: wait, wait, wait – hurry! I read books and I talk about how it all works. I feel I'm now ready to direct. I think I know enough now not to make an ass of myself.

Research, and then more research, is the way Coltrane embarks on any project.

When I was doing the police psychologist in *Cracker* I used to read every single thing that came up in the papers. Five different papers, top to toe, trying to get an insight, find out what the police were expecting, how they were going to catch criminals, were they going to catch them and what their profiles were. You just become obsessed. So with Zukovsky I kept an eye on anything to do with Russia. I read an article the other day saying there's a Russian mob that's moved to New York and the Italians there are pretty frightened of them. If the mob are frightened of them, they must be scary. Did you see *Goodfellas*? What do they do to people in the trunks of cars if the Italian Mob are scared of them?

Coltrane confesses to being 'terribly flattered' that Zukovsky was brought back for the new film.

Somebody told me that they do tests to see if certain characters are liked. It seemed to be a very inorganic thing for the Bond people to do because they're largely instinctive. But I bumped into Barbara and the writers at something and they said they were writing me a really good part for the next Bond. I thought: Yeah, if I got a pound for every time somebody said they were writing me a great part I'd be a very rich man. So I didn't take it very seriously until the script arrived. Then I thought: Great, I get to do lots of leaping around with guns – which I've not done for ages, so that was nice.

Amazingly, on *GoldenEye* Zukovsky appears in only two short scenes. Coltrane recalls:

I was on it for about a day and a half, and one of the big scenes was cut. I was talking to Pierce about it the other day and he was saying it was his first day as Bond and he was very, very nervous. But he didn't appear nervous at all and that's why he's playing Bond – it didn't show. Four years later, though, I can see he's much more at home with the part. We were discussing a scene and I said: 'And then you'll spring up and do a roll-over while picking up the gun and shoot the guy coming through the window. And he didn't say, 'Really?' or 'That's going to be difficult.' He just went: 'Yeah – and then?'

Coltrane fell upon Feirstein's notion of a Sydney Greenstreet-type felon with glee.

I'd always wanted to say lines like, 'Don't be so naïve, Mr Bond.' It was a dream come true. What's interesting about Zukovsky is that it's perfectly realistic to imagine that someone who was flogging second-hand army equipment five years ago in St Petersburg would now have his own casino

BALLOON SEQUENCE

Balloon over Millennium Dome.

Green screen for balloon shot inserts.

Birthday balloon.

Sliceable BMW.

Parahawk.

Jet boat.

Chopper.

France's reserve goalkeeper.

in Baku – the new Klondike. That's the way things have gone. When Russia went over to the so-called free-market economy, the only people who knew how to handle capital were, of course, the hooligans. You didn't have people like Kellogg's and Heinz in Russia. Only people employed by the government – and hooligans. And the hooligans were the people who knew what to do with cash, so they prospered greatly. Gambling and prostitution and things like that are enormous. But I think they've been wise to make Zukovsky legitimate so that he can redeem himself. He's not involved in prostitution and drugs. He does carry a gun and he's not on the right side of the law, but he's not ostensibly a bad man.

Indeed at the end of the film, after Elektra has fired three bullets into his chest and Zukovsky is in his death throes, he saves Bond's life with his dying shot, severing the rope that binds him to the garrotte chair.

Shame that Zukovsky dies, though – it means we won't be seeing him again. Or will we? Michael Wilson reminded me that he had survived being shot in the leg by Bond in an earlier incarnation: 'Maybe his is just a bad chest wound …?' He should leave his soap in the shower.

CHAPTER SIX

RETURN TO PINEWOOD

P rincipal photography on *The World Is Not Enough*
commenced at 8 a.m. on Monday 11 January 1999 on E Stage
at Pinewood Studios, Iver Heath, Buckinghamshire, England.

The first scene consisted of a lethal explosion at the headquarters
of MI6, very much in keeping with Samuel Goldwyn's dictum that his
movies should begin with a volcano erupting and then work their way
up to a climax.

For Michael Wilson and Barbara Broccoli it was a return home
after an odyssey lasting more than ten years. The last Bond film to be
filmed at the studio was *The Living Daylights* with Timothy Dalton

in 1987. The shoot was immortalized by a visit from the Prince and Princess of Wales, when the latter brought down a sugar-glass champagne bottle on her husband's head – a scene captured in a memorable photograph that still hangs in the main stairwell of the studio.

It was found more economic to make most of the next Bond, *Licence To Kill* (1989), in Mexico. And Pinewood was fully booked when *GoldenEye* (1995) started shooting, so a new studio was built at the

Caspian Sea oil walkways created on the back lot Paddock Tank at Pinewood.

Rolls-Royce factory at Leavesden, near Watford. But this was snapped up for *Star Wars* when *Tomorrow Never Dies* (1997) went into production so, with Pinewood again fully booked, they had to build another new studio in an extensive warehouse in Frogmore, in Hertfordshire.

Pinewood, however, is the natural home for a Bond film. The first one, *Dr No*, was made there in 1962 and 14 more, in fairly quick succession, during the next 24 years. Cubby Broccoli kept a permanent office at the studio overlooking the manicured lawns and he built the magnificent 007 Stage there in 1977 for *The Spy Who Loved Me*. It burnt down seven years later but was built again and rededicated in 1984 as the Albert R. Broccoli 007 Stage.

Pinewood Studios nestles in the lanes of bosky Buckinghamshire, 17 miles north-west of London. It was built in 1936 by a property millionaire, Charles Boot, as Britain's answer to America, and it remains the nearest thing in Europe to a Hollywood studio. I remember coming out of the oak-panelled dining room with Christopher Reeve in the summer of 1982 and bumping into Christopher Lambert in the entrance hall. I knew them both but they had never met. It was on my lips to introduce them with the words: 'Tarzan, have you met Superman?' But instead it was: 'Christoph, this is Chris.'

The spirit of Bond dominates the studio, with posters and other mementoes adorning the endless corridors. If one ever wondered of how much interest it is to a member of the public to visit a Bond set, I can quantify the answer exactly. In 1999 there was an auction on a London radio station with the first prize just such a visit, and the bidding went to £3,800 for a morning at the studio. John Parkinson, Pinewood's Senior Vice President of Marketing, had long thought they could, theoretically, turn the set into an active theme park and sell tickets at £50 a head with a queue stretching a mile down the road to the Crooked Billet pub. Even he was surprised by his underestimate. In fact it was Carl Laemmle, the father of the movie theme park, who initiated the tradition, during filming of his silent comedies in the twenties, by selling seats in the bleachers for 25 cents each and charging the punters another 25 cents for a sandwich.

But today movies are shot with sound and much more besides and a Bond set is as tightly guarded as the Pentagon. The first noise a visitor is likely to hear – as he would on approaching any active studio stage – is the sound of hammering. The stand-by carpenters inevitably have some last-minute adjustments to make to the set. And, with this latest Bond, the accompanying noise is that of the gaffer, Kevin Day, shouting to the rigging electricians in the gantry to make the final trims to the lighting set-up.

When the first assistant director, GERRY GAVIGAN, is informed that the set is ready, he passes the information to the director, Michael Apted, and to his assistant directors that they need the actors. Paul Taylor, second assistant, who is stationed down by the stars' dressing rooms and the make-up department, knocks on Pierce Brosnan's door and Paul's team round up the other necessary players.

Some directors – such as Steven Spielberg or Steve Sommers of *The Mummy* – make their presence loudly felt by megaphone, letting everyone know what they hope to achieve from a shot. Michael Apted is more reserved, fingering his chin as he observes the video playback monitors and talking in modulated tones with his producers or stars or Gavigan.

On this set Gerry Gavigan is the sergeant-major who will call the troops into action in his precise Glaswegian voice. Like many on the Bond team, Gavigan is a veteran of a multitude of campaigns, going back 20 years to *Moonraker*, on which he was first assistant on the second unit. He has done seven Bonds in all, five as main unit first

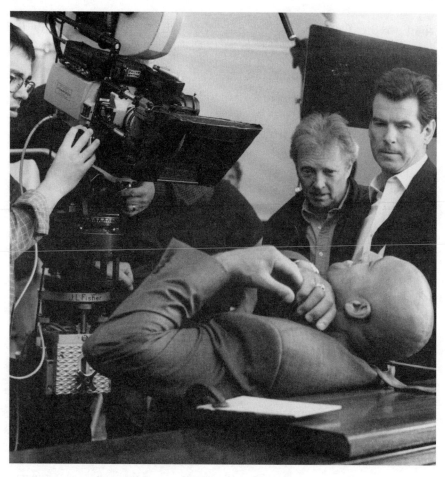

Gerry Gavigan centre checking the action.

assistant, including all three of the Brosnan Bonds. He feels they were very much a change for the better:

The photography was very bland in the early years but Bonds are thrillers and I always thought the photography should have more thriller lighting. Martin Campbell gave it that in *GoldenEye* – and tighter action. Roger Spottiswoode had a strong vision of what he wanted in *Tomorrow Never Dies* and I think he got it. Michael Apted is much more interested in the actors and the storyline.

Gavigan's role began long before shooting. The first assistant had to schedule the working days for all the actors – no easy task when Dame Judi Dench was lost to America after the first three weeks. Bond films cannot be shot chronologically, so, for instance, Denise Richards's scientist, Dr Christmas Jones, went through months of hell with Bond as they avoided bullets, fireballs and giant helicopter saws before being introduced to him for the first time on location in Zaragoza in Spain. Bobby Carlyle vouchsafed to me that, with several weeks between his scenes, he lived in fear of losing his Serbian accent – although he knew he could always postsynch it. However, Chris Munro, the experienced sound mixer, reported that the voice matched perfectly. Gavigan also had to dovetail his schedule with that of Terry Madden, now doing Gerry's old job on the second unit, as actors moved between the two units.

Phil Meheux and Robert Elswit having given the Brosnan Bonds a distinctive modern look, Michael Apted needed a Director of Photography (DoP) who would be fast and maintain that standard. ADRIAN BIDDLE, an Oscar nominee for *Thelma And Louise,* had never worked with Apted before but his reputation went before him. As well as having a prestigious career in commercials, Biddle worked on features as a focus puller but never became a camera operator – the usual step between that and DoP. However, when James 'Titanic' Cameron was in Britain directing *Aliens* he fired his DoP at the end of the first week of shooting and on the Sunday met Biddle, who started his new career as a DoP on Monday morning.

A taciturn man, Biddle tends not to give interviews, keeping the secrets of his art close to his chest. But we were well acquainted with each other, having spent a long, hot summer together on *Fierce Creatures* (also at Pinewood), so when I slapped my tape-recorder on

Director of Photography Adrian Biddle.

top of the book he was reading (*Stalingrad*), he had the good grace not
to push it away.

'It's good to have a Bond film under your belt,' he acknowledged:

The director can choose his own editor and cameraman. These films have
got huge budgets, so you're allowed an awful lot of light. There's no need
to compromise. I always think the bigger the set is, the easier it is to light.
So with the walkways on the Paddock Tank we had plenty of room to work,
and all round the set we had little fibre-optic lights which could be stars or
other walkways sparkling in the distance.

Once a set begins to be built you can see what the lighting should be. In
the nuclear facility on the 007 Stage, Michael Apted wanted it to have a gritty,
run-down sort of look. In the interior of the submarine there was no room for
film lights, so you put in souped-up practicals [lights that the audience can see].

Biddle had no problem with the way he lit his stars. 'Pierce has been around long enough to know that you know what you're doing. He came to rushes the first few days and didn't find 'anything to worry about. And there were no requests from any of the leading women. I just like to get a light in their eyes for close-ups. I didn't get any instructions from them – unlike on some films,' he remarked with a telling smile.

Bond's dialogue on that first day consisted of two words: 'Stop! King!', so the emphasis was on the action. More than £3 million in banknotes was due to explode – or appear to explode – so the risk assessment carried out by Chris Corbould, the special-effects supervisor, required closer reading than any script.

"BOND 19"

Assessment No.	6	
Assessment by ;	Chris Corbould	
Assessment date ;	04/01/98	
Date of shot/test	Testing 04/01/98 - 08/01/98 Shooting 11/01/98 - 13/01/98	
Location	E - Stage, Pinewood Studios - Int. MI6	
Description/Effect	Effect of explosion from banknotes using pyrotechnics and flammable substances	
	Effect of trolley flying through the air using compressed air and hitting glass doors	
	Effect of debris flying through the air using air mortars	
	Effect of suspended ceiling collapsing from explosion	YES
		YES
Hazards	Risk of injury from flying debris	YES
	Risk of burns from heat and flame generated	YES
	Risk of damage to hearing	YES
	Risk of accidental ignition of flammables/pyrotechnics	YES
	Risk of radio frequencies initiating pyrotechnics	
	Risk of secondary objects catching fire from explosion	YES
	Risk of inhalation of smoke and fumes	YES
	Risk of personnel being hit by flying trolley	YES
	Risk of glass doors shattering from trolley impact	

It is a commonplace to compare a film crew at work to a military operation – although in movies nobody puts their lives at risk – but the director is very much the Brigadier commanding his Brigade with a variety of resources at his command. (The producers may be regarded as General HQ.) Adrian Biddle and the camera operator, Dave Worley, are the director's eyes. You get the sense that if Dave feels another angle might work better or a crane shot should end up in a different place he is not slow to respectfully offer an alternative.

Apted's ears are CHRIS MUNRO, the most innovative sound mixer in the British business. No muffed line or extraneous noise passes through his headphones unnoted. It used to be that sound on a film was recorded on quarter-inch tape and then transferred to 35mm magnetic stock to be synchronized in the cutting room and shown double system – with the magnetically recorded sound on a separate reel from the picture – at the daily 'rushes' where the preferred takes were shown.

Not with Chris. Knowing the Bond has a perilously short post-production period compared with most films of this scale – say eight weeks as against eight months – he records the sound digitally on a DAT (digital audio tape) that carries all the information about each shot and this tape goes straight into the AVID editing machine. At daily rushes a digital dubber provides first-generation sound which is matched to the clapperboard.

Munro says:

To me making films is seeing rushes on film, not video. It's good for every department to see the film in the same form it will be seen by the public. All the sound is under my control. It used to be very fashionable to use ADR [Automatic Dialogue Replacement] on a lot of the dialogue – some directors thought they could improve performances in ADR – but we're providing Michael with first-class sound which will keep its quality all the way through post-production and we have a pretty professional cast.

Munro's state-of-the art system goes in tandem with Nikki Clapp, the script supervisor (known as the 'continuity girl' in non-PC days), who still notes down the takes the director wants to print with that old-fashioned instrument a pen, although every time she has a moment she's seated by her Apple laptop punching in Chris's co-ordinates.

By far the biggest regiment at Brigadier Apted's disposal is the Art Department under PETER LAMONT. The 'Lieutenant Colonel' has a staff that expands and contracts according to demand, but at full strength it numbers more than 400 men and women.

More than anybody else working at Pinewood on Monday 11 January 1999, Lamont is a veteran graduate of the Bond University. He has worked on 14 of the 19 films, starting with *Goldfinger* (1964) and would have done *Tomorrow Never Dies* had it not been for the fact that, as he says, 'I didn't want to leave a sinking ship.' It was a prudent decision. He won the 1998 Academy Award for his work as Production Designer on James Cameron's *Titanic*.

Lamont makes no secret of his indebtedness to Ken Adam, his old boss, who designed the first seven Bonds. Today's MI6 set is largely sliding glass doors and corridors and since few of us – except Judi Dench – have been inside the Secret Service, it is a conception based on what is known of this modern structure, incorporating the right trappings of computer technology. But after the building has been put out of service by the exploding money, Dame Judi and her team move to Thane Castle in the Scottish Highlands. The exterior was filmed at Eilean Donan Castle, a place for which Lamont confesses he has long had a soft spot.

Oscar-winning production designer Peter Lamont – not a man to leave a sinking ship.

'Having worked with Ken for so long,' Lamont explains, 'I don't want to cheat the public with wood-grained paper. We've built the interior out of oak. It doesn't cost much more for the real thing – in fact it saves on labour.' (True to this tradition, Lamont built the dining room and staircase on *Titanic* out of oak – and the set was broken up after the film. As an artefact it could have been an internationally popular attraction, although they weren't to know that at the time.)

Once the director was on board, Lamont joined him, Michael Wilson, Adrian Biddle and Anthony Waye, the line producer, on a location scout. They started in Istanbul, where the famous Maiden's Tower, on an island in the middle of the Bosporus, was to play a pivotal role in the plot. It was a part of the world that had already found favour with Bond movies – Terence Young had shot *From Russia With Love* (1963) there.

Nobody, however, had filmed a Bond in Azerbaijan and when they got there they found out why. The oil platforms that they had seen in Barbara's television programme were up to 50 miles out to sea. 'We flew out in a helicopter to a huge gas field where Russians had built this weird staging,' Lamont recalls. 'Some of it was derelict, some of it falling into the sea but still working.'

However, with a putrid smell of raw oil and gas in the air, he knew they would never be able to bring a large unit there. A company offered to build a tank in Turkey beside the ocean in Antaria, but Lamont decided there was no decent infrastructure to get people and materials to the location. So he built a model and, on the basis of this, transformed the Paddock Tank on the back lot at Pinewood into a section of the Caspian Sea containing a vast oil platform and caviar factory. 'It was 400 feet long, 300 feet wide and 60 feet high. We used over 25 miles of timber, 2,500 sheets of quarter-inch ply and

356 miles of tubing. We also used about 300 old telegraph poles which we got at a fraction of their price from British Telecom, who were renewing some old stock.'

For the nuclear facility Lamont watched a lot of documentary material about Russian underground cities.

Only during surveillance by Americans did they find these places – they could tell from the sky that some rivers were radiating. There was one city where they would only let old people underground because it was so radioactive. If young people had been there their lifespan would have been shortened. We built the tunnels based loosely on the way the Channel Tunnel was built and our master plasterer came up with a format to give a rotting effect to the concrete. A lot of the old Soviet complexes are now falling to pieces because they economized with the cement. The painters got in there and made the entire set look wet and slimy, as if it had been degenerating for many years. I had to come up with ideas. I've got a book called Secret Places In East Germany in which there were amazing nuclear bunkers. There was a sequence where they wanted Bond to escape through closing steel iris doors. But these are very difficult to make and [it would be] difficult to time Bond escaping through them. But in the book they had one particular door that could be divided into four elements with the sides closing in and then the top and bottom closing in. So you could get the effect of an iris without an iris.

Within the nuclear facility Dr Christmas Jones is required to deactivate the nuclear element from the plutonium core of a bomb. So Lamont's department was obliged to learn how to make one. A government scientist came down to Pinewood and gave them a lecture. He chalked a series of equations on a blackboard – 'All except the last one,' recalls Concept Stylist Robert Cowper, 'which would have

STORYBOARDS

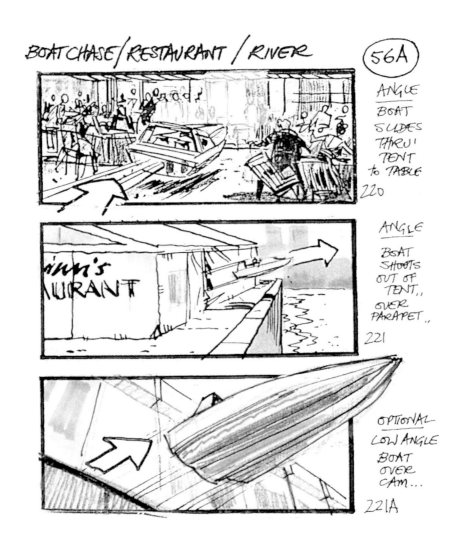

BOAT CHASE / RESTAURANT / RIVER   (56A)

ANGLE
BOAT SLIDES THRU TENT to TABLE
220

ANGLE
BOAT SHOOTS OUT OF TENT,, OVER PARAPET,,
221

OPTIONAL LOW ANGLE BOAT OVER CAM...
221A

BOAT CHASE/RESTAURANT/RIVER (57)

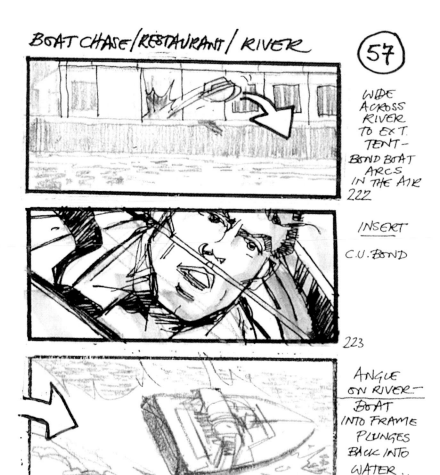

WIDE
ACROSS
RIVER
TO EXT.
TENT —
BOND BOAT
ARCS
IN THE AIR
222

INSERT

C.U. BOND

223

ANGLE
ON RIVER —
BOAT
INTO FRAME
PLUNGES
BACK INTO
WATER...
223

BOAT CHASE

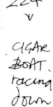

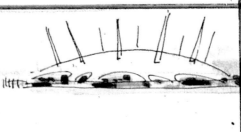

CUTAWAY
C.U.
CIGAR
GIRL.

|
224
∨

CIGAR
BOAT.
racing
down
INDIA &
MILLWALL
Dock
225

CIGAR
BOAT
EXITS
INDIA &
MILLWALL
DOCK
PAN ⟩ with her
To find DOME

226

Chopper Attack.

(21)

BOND
POV.
HELICOPTER
MOVING OVER
AND DROPPING
DOWN OTHER
SIDE OF
CAVIAR
74   FACTORY

CUT

C.U.
BOND
WATCHING

75   CUT

SUDDENLY !

<u>INSERT</u>

SPINNING
BLADE
CRASHES
THRU' ROOF
OF CAR.

76   CUT

SHOCKED
BOND
IN EX. C.U.
F.G. RIGHT

WHIRRING
SAW
MOVING
TOWARD
HIM IN BG.

77 .

CAVIAR FACTORY

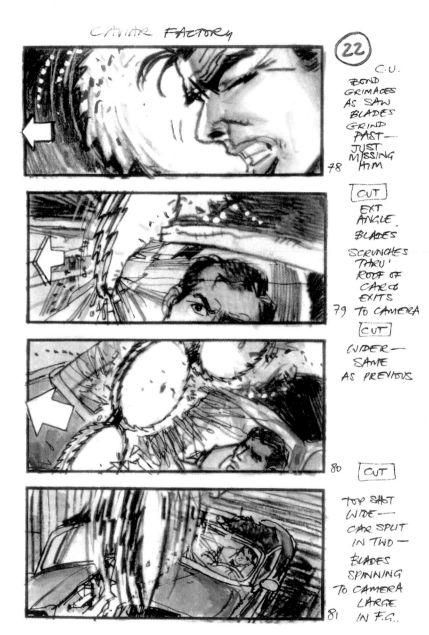

(22)

C.U.
BOND
GRIMACES
AS SAW
BLADES
GRIND
PAST—
JUST
MISSING
78 HIM

CUT
EXT
ANGLE.
BLADES
SCRUNCHES
THRU'
ROOF OF
CAR &
EXITS
79 TO CAMERA

CUT
WIDER—
SAME
AS PREVIOUS

80 CUT

TOP SHOT
WIDE—
CAR SPLIT
IN TWO—
BLADES
SPINNING
TO CAMERA
LARGE
81 IN F.G..

(23)

ANGLE
ON BOND
GAUGING
DISTANCE

82 CUT

LOW ANGLE
HIS P.O.V.
RECEEDING
HELICOPTER

83 CUT

EX.
C.U.
BOND

84 CUT

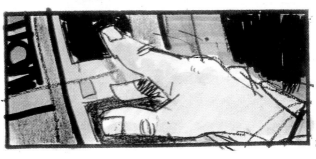

INSERT
HIS FINGER
STABS
FIRING
BUTTON.

85

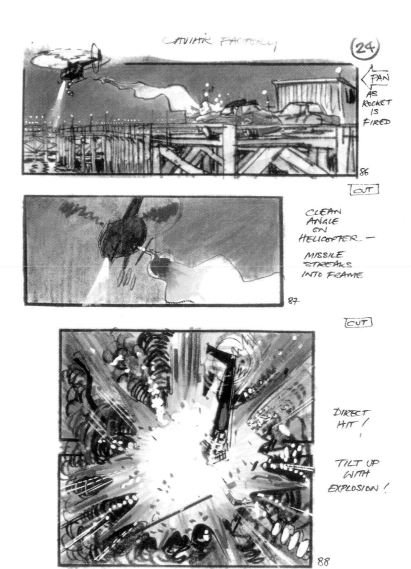

CAVIAR FACTORY

(24)

PAN AS ROCKET IS FIRED

86

CUT

CLEAN ANGLE ON HELICOPTER —

MISSILE STREAKS INTO FRAME

87

CUT

DIRECT HIT !

TILT UP WITH EXPLOSION !

88

shown us how to really make one.' In Bond films there is a tradition of trying to make both the stunts and scenery as near real as possible – but when it comes to nuclear bombs a little dramatic licence is permitted: aluminium for plutonium.

CHAPTER SEVEN

ON LOCATION

It's 6.30 on a freezing morning early in February in the fashionable French ski resort of Chamonix, nestling beneath the dominating majesty of Mont Blanc. This was where the first Winter Olympics took place, in 1924. (This was also the year that Paris played host to the memorable summer games portrayed in *Chariots Of Fire*, when Eric Liddell turned his back on a gold medal because he refused to run on a Sunday.)

But no skiers have even stirred in their slumber yet. Indeed the 150 or so muffled figures decanting themselves into four-wheel drives and minibuses are expressly forbidden to ski by their employers – unless it is part of their job.

They make their way across the Salange valley and up the side of the Duran mountain range opposite. At Burzier, the first base camp, elongated catering wagons supply a welcome breakfast of bacon and fried eggs, baked beans and sausages, which people eat on paper plates with plastic forks, all the while stamping their feet to maintain their circulation.

In strict order of precedence (camera crews first) people mount the 432s – chained vehicles hired from the Swiss Army – to make their way up the next stage of the mountain to Camp Two: La Ferme de Tournieux – a refuge, judging from the pictures on the wall, that used only to be attainable on a sled pulled by huskies. Supplied by the kitchen, scalding coffee pumps new adrenalin into the system.

The time is now 7.52 a.m. and a wonderful rose-red hue tinges the mountains and there, across the valley, is the unforgettable beauty of Mont Blanc at sunrise. But the wonder of the moment is broken by the angry revving of a line of snowmobiles waiting to ferry people to the top of the glacier.

It's 12,000 feet and you wonder whether it is altitude or age that makes breathing less than easy – probably a bit of both. The dawn has passed and the snow here is sometimes ice-green, sometimes ice-blue – unspoiled and ethereal. Well, not quite unspoiled. Two Panavision cameras are already nestling in their scooped bunkers and, bisecting a line between them some 160 feet higher up, an imperceptible slope has been built as a safe landing for skiers.

VIC ARMSTRONG, the second-unit director, turns to his meteorologist for a weather check. There seems to be hardly any wind, but in fact it is just below the permitted force for a helicopter to hover at this height. Vic gives the go-ahead into his walkie-talkie. Jonathan Taylor, the DoP, responds with a thumbs-up and the camera crews and sound recordist, Ian Munro, wielding a grey tufted boom-mike, stand by for the shot.

Seven minutes later the early-morning silence is broken once again by two Squirrel BS helicopters cutting through the crisp, clear mountain air. The second of them hangs back – it is there for emergency and safety purposes. The cameras roll and the first helicopter crabs towards them. A door slides open and as it hovers ten feet above the glacier, the unmistakable figures of Elektra King and James Bond stylishly leap down on to the unbroken snow and shoot expertly off down the mountain.

Once well clear of the cameras, the couple skid to a stop and waiting snowmobiles pull them back up the hill to the director's position behind the main camera. Vic congratulates the two stars on their performance and Francine Moreillon and Stéphan Dan accept their good notices but insist they can do it more smoothly. They may not be the accepted stars of this movie – Sophie Marceau and Pierce Brosnan have that honour – but they are stars and world champions in their own field of Extreme Skiing, a worldwide sport for the intrepid that has its origins and headquarters here in Chamonix.

I asked Stéphan to define it for me and he replied: 'It is skiing where you don't fall over.' Which is a modest way of saying that if you do fall they pick up you up in pieces at the bottom of the mountain.

Championships are now shown on television – I had seen Francine in a competition at Crested Butte, Colorado, the previous week. The ultimate example of this mad art is *The Man Who Skied Down Everest*. But the top Extreme Skiers whom the stunt co-ordinator, SIMON CRANE, had selected for the Alpine sequence were more than daredevils – they were expert guides who knew the rocks, crevasses and other hazards of Mont Blanc and the surrounding mountains like the back of their hand.

Simon had used the same criteria in selecting them as he did when selecting his own regular stunt team. 'Stunt men are employed to minimize risk, not to take it. We picked world-class Extreme Skiers with the best attitude. Also, they had to understand English because I can't speak French. Safety is paramount.'

The ski chase is meant to be taking place in the Caucasus Mountains between the Caspian and Black Seas, where Elektra is showing Bond the route for her new oil pipeline. Nobody in the second unit seemed much concerned whether Brosnan or Sophie Marceau could actually ski. (Sophie later told me she'd done a little in her childhood and proved surprisingly adept when she came out to do her inserts.) Of more concern were the costumes. Whatever the doubles wore would be the outfits for the stars. Vic had asked Michael Apted what Sophie might favour and was informed that she was 'manifesting her nerves through her choice of costume at present'. So the second-unit director found a saucy postcard in a Chamonix shop of

a female naked except for her ski boots and suggested to Michael that
he might like to show this to his star. The director is believed to
have demurred.

However, Lindy Hemming, the costume designer, thought Elektra
might be more at home in a trim wine Versace one-piece with a
artificial fur headband, whereas Pierce was in olive green, his double
wearing a black wig to match the star's hair.

An initial script had Bond and Elektra being chased through the
trees by Renard's gun-toting thugs. But Simon Crane had recently
been on a parachute holiday and seen an old-fashioned paraglider.
He thought it might be fun if Bond's oppressors came out of the
air like Valkyries. 'We're always looking for something new,'
he said, 'but the parahawks I saw weren't quite right, so we
designed our own, all black with smaller canopies so that we
could get tighter turns and bigger engines.' There was a problem

when the craft landed – their aerodynamics being different from those of normal skidoos – but rapid engineering and extra weight on the front ski made them fast and manoeuvrable on the snow.

Thus the Bond Brigade Airforce Division is lined up on a mountain-top slope for the next three weeks, five mean-looking black parahawks (four to fly and one in reserve), armed with cannons and grenades, and black silk parachutes spread out behind. One pilot, the American Tim Le Blanc, has experience of similar ultra-light machines but Crane's stunt men are mainly ex-Paratroopers and champing at the bit to launch themselves off a cliff into thousands of feet of nothingness. The parahawks are unnaturally heavy, so they have to take off downwind and are then steered with the feet. A week's training in Florida has ironed out some of the problems, but it doesn't stop one of them landing across the valley at Argentier Heliport and the back-up Squirrel being unable to go to pick it up until French transit authorities fill out the paperwork for the helicopter to cross the main highway.

Such irritations overcome, the scene is set for a chase to the death in which these birds of prey turn the mountainside into an exploding battlefield in their endeavour to obliterate the slaloming British agent.

The scene will be captured by a battery of cameras on the ground and, from the point of view of the parahawks, lipstick cameras integrated in their fuselage as in the Grand Prix cars we see on television. There is still a considerable debate as to whether these images will blow up satisfactorily to a Panavision size – maybe they will for a split second – but there is no doubt that Emmanuel Préviner's mini-helicopter with its flying eyeball will provide some of the most spectacular swooping shots in the sequence – the Belgian device has already won a Hollywood Oscar and is a big favourite with Vic Armstrong.

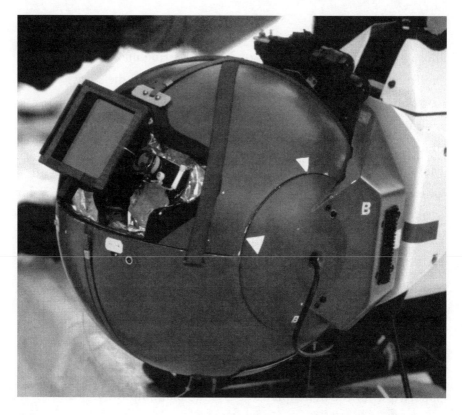

The flying eyeball.

The second-unit director seems confidently at home in the Alps. He has done this sort of stuff before:

What I need is unmarked snow and a rugged look – not somewhere round the corner from St Moritz. As long as I don't get chalets and ski marks in I'm all right. The film crew could be Kurd shepherds with dodgy hats on if they get in shot. Any chase should last four and a half minutes – five minutes and you start wriggling in your seat. You've got to look at it like music – not too many explosions or bullet hits. You don't want a three-course meal of salmon, salmon and salmon. You've got to vary it.

Armstrong has a 170-strong crew shooting for four weeks for his four and a half minutes. He manages to shoot from 8.30 a.m. to 4.30 p.m. Each shot takes on average an hour with multiple cameras. What he defines as a 'pretty shot' with the right sun and scenery can take four to five hours. This is short by the standards of the storm sequence that Armstrong worked on for David Lean in *Ryan's Daughter* – that took five months to get right. 'That's what movies are about,' he smiles.

Compact and confident, Armstrong is something of a contrast to Michael Apted, for whom he works and with whom he has a good working relationship. 'Michael wouldn't have got as far as he has in Hollywood without a bright mind and a good story sense,' he acknowledges.

Armstrong and Apted.

In fact Armstrong was employed to direct the second unit before the main director came on board – just as he had done on *GoldenEye* and *Tomorrow Never Dies*. Whereas Apted will cogitate about a series of options, Armstrong has no doubts when he has finally nailed the image he wants. 'It's like poker: you've got to know when to hold them, know when to fold them. When you've got the shot you've just got to walk away.'

He understands stunt men because he was the number one himself, learning his trade with Ridley Scott on commercials. He doubled Sean Connery in *You Only Live Twice*, dropping into a volcano, and learned to ski for *On Her Majesty's Secret Service,* where he doubled George Lazenby. The stunt co-ordinator for the memorable cable-car escape was George Leech, father of Armstrong's wife Wendy, herself a stunt woman. On the Schiltorn mountain Armstrong learned the necessity of hot and cold running food. For the Chamonix shoot he rounded up expert snowboarders (an unheard of sport 20 years previously) and fitted them out with Swiss Army thermal backpacks. This meant that there was a constant supply of soup, glühwein, steak sandwiches, Mars Bars and more – in fact anything that could be eaten with gloves on in 20 degrees below – throughout the day, thereby gaining up to two valuable hours that could otherwise be lost to a lunch break.

A mark of Armstrong's international reputation is the fact that he was stunt co-ordinator and doubled Harrison Ford on all the Indiana Jones films. He has more than one feature under his belt, having directed Jean-Claude Van Damme in *Double Impact*, and is fiercely protective of his territory. 'What is a Bond? Look at the trailers – they give the movie's pulse. Why did we make it? What's going to attract people? Action–action–sex–action. It's worth an extravagant expenditure of money – although we have to fight for it.'

Simon Crane in stunt discussion.

Simon Crane, with a lean athlete's body and permanent tan and grin, used to be part of Armstrong's team. He stunt-doubled for Timothy Dalton on *The Living Daylights* and *Licence To Kill*, going on to co-ordinate on *GoldenEye*. He would have done *Tomorrow Never Dies*, but, like Peter Lamont, did not want to leave a sinking ship. Working with James Cameron on *Titanic*, Crane found himself with up to 120 stunt men . He remembers the day when the call sheet required 6,000 people, most of whom were going to go over the side – his most pressing task was to stop Cameron from joining them.

Given his work on that and the inspired verisimilitude of his sequences in *Saving Private Ryan*, I suggested to Crane that maybe there should be an Oscar for stunt co-ordinators. He thought probably not. 'You wouldn't want it for Best Stunt because you'd get great competition and people would be killing themselves left, right and centre. But you could get it for Best Action Sequence. It would give us some kind of recognition in cases where the action makes or breaks a film.'

Then, in a terrible Act of God, on Wednesday February 10th a completely unpredictable avalanche swept away 17 chalets.

The Bond location immediately closed down and diverted its emergency services and personnel and two Squirrel helicopters to help in the aftermath. A few people got out alive but lasting damage was inflicted by the mountain.

A vast avalanche sequence to conclude the parahawk chase was not shot but Bond and Elektra still end up buried under a snowfall and likely to suffocate were it not for Bond's ballooning jacket courtesy of Q's department.

But this was first-unit work. Mara Bryan, the visual effects supervisor, flew out to Chamonix specially to take the lighting information of the master shot of the slope under which they are buried. 'I draw up maps, take a compass reading, note the time of day, take stills and I've got a little ball that looks like a toilet cistern that I hold up in front of the camera so you can see how the light hits it. Then, when they build a closer shot of the slope in Pinewood, we can match it exactly.'

Another Q device is to prove Bond's salvation in the traditional big number that opens the movie – in this instance a chase up the River Thames from MI6 slightly west of the Houses of Parliament to the new Millennium Dome just upstream from the Thames Barrier.

Q's later protestation that Bond had 'borrowed' and trashed a fishing boat that he had been preparing for his retirement must be taken with a pinch of salt, given that the model that burst through the gaping hole in MI6's wall was a jet boat capable of speeds up to 40 knots.

Simon Crane had seen Bentz boats racing on a television programme and convinced Barbara Broccoli that they would provide his team with some fun on the movie. Before that she had to be persuaded that the Thames would be a good location. The initiative came with the London Film Commission, who thought it was about time that Bond put his native city back on the map. As a result, the producers and directors were invited on a cruise to assess the new-look river front. It proved enticing and the riparian landowners and councils proved cooperative and Chris Livett, the Thames waterman conducting the pitch, delivered the coup de grâce when he showed them the foundations of the Millennium Dome, which would be in good shape in time for the shoot.

Even MI6 didn't mind them filming their building – but they drew the line at having a hole blasted in its riverside wall. So a model exterior of the Secret Service building was built on the back lot at Pinewood and miniature-effects supervisor John Richardson blew a mighty hole in that instead. Vic Armstrong had a slipway constructed to the lee of the real MI6 headquarters and it was from this that Bond's jet boat was fired, accelerating from 0 to 60 knots in about one second flat.

Thus the Bond Navy took to the Thames in a novel version of the Boat Race. The Cigar Girl, in her twin-engine 350cc 42-foot Sunseeker with her Heckler & Koch G36 rifle and mounted 21 hybrid belt-fed gun, plus a 12-bore self-loading shotgun, a Smith and Wesson MOD 469 9mm ten-shot semi-automatic rifle and a limitless supply of depth-charges, races away from Bond, who is in a slower jet boat with a Walther P99. The odds seem unfair.

When they began the shoot-out outside the Secret Service building a member of the public telephoned a local paper and a junior reporter was sent to investigate this possible assault on MI6. But the police knew about it already. In fact they, too, had had a 999 call but Chris Livett, in his role as liaison officer, had informed the Thames Division of the Metropolitan Police at 7 a.m. every morning of what the filming plans were.

When the chase reached the House of Commons, one of the Parliamentary Committees sitting that morning issued a complaint about the gunfire.

'What did we do?' enquired Livett, a man with a droll sense of humour. 'Wake them up?' In fact it turned out that it was pile-drivers on the government-commissioned Millennium Ferris wheel that were making the noise.

For the helicopter shot that established the chase involving the two boats and pursuing police launches between Vauxhall and Tower Bridge, a mile of the Thames had to be closed off. First Livett needed to clear the river of driftwood and then position Port of London Authority launches at either end to keep this stretch of water clear.

Vic Armstrong had done boat chases before and didn't want a conventional pursuit like the one through Amsterdam in *Puppet On A Chain*. The Sunseeker could clearly outpace the jet boat but Simon had discovered that the latter could travel in six inches of water, so it didn't take long to adapt a version that could travel in no inches of water.

If you look at the Thames in an aerial photograph, it can be seen to make a substantial loop, a feature familiar to television viewers from the opening sequence of the BBC's *EastEnders*. This is maybe not a programme Bond would be addicted to, but his extensive knowledge of London would make him aware of a short cut through Tobacco Wharf, down a narrow street, through a fish market, a few more quick turns and then back on to the Thames a couple of miles downstream. Well worth a detour.

This scene is the artistic invention of the film-makers rather than any landlubber writers, and moments such as his bursting through a fashionable fish restaurant or drenching two wheel-clampers at work come from the tongue-in-cheek style of men steeped in Bond lore.

Since the Cigar Girl has considerably more fire-power than Bond, he turns his craft into a human missile to take out her main armament.

Tests on Hawley Reservoir found that it was impossible to somersault the boat off a ramp as could be done with a car. However, Simon Crane and his crew discovered that by adding Vickers air mortars to the fuselage they could rotate the jet boat on a crane and so choreographed a barrel roll that removed the Sunseeker's machine-gun and much else besides.

For the less outrageous parts of the chase, Brosnan himself took the controls of the boat. 'It was enormous fun,' he recalled, 'and a great challenge to go like the clappers down the river and no-brain yourself on Lambeth Bridge or something like that. It takes it out of you on the legs. In the morning I was James Bond but in the afternoon it was back to Pierce Brosnan.'

Crane also discovered that if you put the jet boat into reverse at 60mph you plummeted under the water, and so he enclosed the engine to make the craft submerge and later emerge. Against ingenuity like this the Cigar Girl had problems. She does, however, manage to blast a schooner out of the water, drop depth-charges in the Royal Victoria Dock, crash through a crowded landing stage and a police vessel blocking her path, causing a nearby yachting fuel station to explode.

The Cigar Girl makes her getaway.

Just when she sees salvation from her persistent pursuer by shooting her way into a cross-Channel balloon race, a final leap by Bond allows him to shin up the rope to her basket before she falls victim to her own master.

The final section with balloon and helicopters relied on inserted model and CGI (computer-generated image) shots, but Pierce Brosnan will go down in history as the first person to land on the Millennium Dome.

The third major location sequence took place within the confines of the studio on the specially enlarged Paddock Tank. This was where Azerbaijan comes to Pinewood and both first and second units worked alternate weeks of winter nights to accomplish it.

The sequence saw the realization of a long-harboured dream of the producer Michael Wilson. Many years ago B. J. Worth, one of the main skydivers in the Bond series since 1979's *Moonraker,* brought him a tape of helicopters with giant chain-saws suspended beneath them which are the only means of lopping branches from trees that encroach on power lines in parts of the USA and Canada. Wilson liked the idea of using one but pointed out to me:

There are two issues that always come up in a narrative story – one is, somewhere in the story, you have to see it doing its natural job and then when you see it, it has to be part of the story and not completely gratuitous. Since we're building a pipeline here, it would be a good opportunity to have the saws cutting the rights of way for the pipeline. Now you have to say what you're going to do with it and, of course, attacking Bond in the caviar factory at night seems like a kind of perfect thing to do.

The helicopter saw had actually been in the original script for *GoldenEye* and special-effects supervisor CHRIS CORBOULD had spent two months preparing one. 'It was a headache then,' he remembered, 'and a great feeling when they decided to cut it out. There was no sign of it in *Tomorrow Never Dies* and Peter Lamont sent me the script for this one and I picked it up and there was the bloody saw-blade – five times as long as it was in *GoldenEye*. It turned out to be the biggest and most technical operation of the movie.'

Corbould, a youthful figure with close-cropped dark hair, has been on the Bond team since *Moonraker*. He made an impression on the assembled British Film Industry in 1996, when he spoke movingly at the Celebration of the Life and Work of Cubby Broccoli.

He knew Wilson wanted his cherished walkway-slicing sequence to work for real. To begin with they found there wasn't enough torque in the chain-saw engine to cut through test materials, so it was beefed up with a high-powered motorcycle engine. Corbould explained that:

Even so, every product it cuts though is carefully moulded in lightweight fabrics and materials. When it cuts through the BMW car it is effectively two halves with a whole middle section made from foils and lightweight substitutes – we can't cut through steel. And we made four major cuts through the factory. In the first we dropped the whole corner of the factory away and then we cut the whole side wall out.

Sliced BMW

The bottom half of the helicopter was suspended from a vast crane completely computerized on the biggest motion-control rig most of those present had ever seen. Local residents would not permit flying at night. So the shots from the tank looking up at the Bell helicopters were done at Aldershot later.

Like every action sequence in the film, the required shots were storyboarded by Martin Asbury. 'We take the script and our job is to show the most exciting way of doing something,' he explained to me. 'People say, "You can't do that."' Then you find out how you can. Originally you didn't see the car being sliced in half but I felt the audience would be cheated if they didn't actually see it.'

On the walkways with units swapping over and stunt doubles and Pierce and Denise alternating in sections of sequences, some kind of order was preserved by reference to this original blueprint.

As Apted was shooting on the walkways, his second unit was working on the river. He recalled:

I had a very bizarre experience early on. I was very troubled by a scene I was going to shoot on the river chase and I went early one morning to the labs to look at the second-unit rushes and there was the scene I had been fretting about. I thought: Shit – I didn't realize they were going to do that. But I looked at my schedule and sure enough it was on it. It was my own negligence and it was a kind of wake-up call. I realized that an important part of this job is knowing exactly what everybody else is doing – second, third and model units – and making sure they're doing what I want or stuff is going to fall by the wayside.

CHAPTER EIGHT

SOLVING PROBLEMS

There was a confident atmosphere on the set of *The World Is Not Enough* but behind the scenes the film was confronted with non-stop problems.

The first was this: MGM/UA, who were financing the movie, didn't care for the initial script. Michael Apted recalls: 'The studio was putting us under a fair amount of pressure because they didn't very much like the initial script. They sort of approved of the story but I think we realized quite early on that this was not going to be the end of the story.'

Accordingly Dana Stevens, Apted's wife, was brought in to work on the central story between Pierce and Sophie and the other female parts. But that took too much emphasis away from the star. Apted acknowledges: 'Pierce didn't really like Dana's writing very much because he thought he was being short-changed by it.'

Accordingly Bruce Feirstein (and later Michael Wilson) were working on rewrites many months into shooting. If this wasn't enough for Wilson, he and Barbara Broccoli were preoccupied with another problem. They filed a law suit against Sony, the Hollywood studio who were threatening to make a Bond of their own. The situation wasn't resolved until halfway through shooting.

Another equally serious problem for the film was the fact that a great deal of the story was set in Turkey, especially Istanbul and the Cappadocia region – but they couldn't shoot in Turkey. The Kurdish rebel group the PKK, whose captured leader, Abdullah Ocalan, was on trial when the main unit was meant to be in the country, had threatened to target all tourists and their desire to get worldwide headline coverage for their cause would be easily accomplished if they attacked a Bond film. Accordingly James Bond – in the persona of Pierce Brosnan – never set foot in Turkey.

So at dead of night on Thursday 1 April 1999 – unknown to virtually everyone else at Pinewood – a 12-man unit secretly flew to Istanbul to take some establishing shots of a movie called 'Destiny'. They split into three camera teams. Most of the filming was done at dawn or dusk and at one stage they had two cameras shooting in Europe and one in Asia, the Bosporus Strait being the dividing line between the continents. Local people had been selected as stand-ins, bringing to 11 the number of men who would play James Bond in this picture: three in Turkey, two Extreme Skiers (Stéphan Dan and Yan André), two boat drivers (Gary Powell and Wade Eastwood), his two regular stunt doubles (Mark Mottram and Mark Southwood) and a man in Azerbaijan.

Azerbaijan presented its own problem, which was largely solved by the Paddock Tank set, but they had to get Zukovsky's Rolls-Royce to the real oil walkway – some 50 miles out to sea in the Caspian. The only means of transport were ancient Russian MI8 helicopters and landing after dark in these did not prove to be everybody's favourite trip.

The Paddock Tank walkways provided their own problems as the first unit shot on them for six weeks and the second unit for two weeks. But the second unit had to be pulled off the Thames and the first unit was shooting on the underground nuclear facility on the 007 Stage, and since both these sets were being methodically destroyed – the walkways being chopped up by the helicopter saws – and it took two days to move the helicopter crane from angle to angle, the logistics proved a little complicated.

Line producer Anthony Waye, on analysing the script, estimated that it would take 20 weeks to shoot. That's 100 working days. In fact it wrapped on the hundred-and-ninth day – an overrun of less than 10 per cent. Waye told me: 'Bonds generally balance out. You initially have a construction team of 300–400 people, a special effects team of

50, two cameras on the first unit and two on the second, you're bound to have a camera crane each day and you have to allow 100 flying hours for a helicopter – we probably had 2,000 people employed at some stage overall at home and abroad.'

And the budget? Movie producers rarely reveal how much their films cost. But it's a logical guesstimate that this is a $100-million Bond. And one can probably add at least another $50–75 million for producing international prints and advertising.

Set against this is the fact that the last two Bonds grossed nearly $800 million worldwide and the ones before didn't do so badly either. The films of the late seventies and early eighties were chalking up close to $200 million each internationally and these figures can be doubled if index-linked to today's values. These films are not a licence to print money, but they are not a licence to lose it either. The Bond library sells consistently on television around the world. The returns are impossible to estimate, but an annual income of up to $20 million might not be far wide of the mark. ITV recently paid $5 million for the first TV showing of *Tomorrow Never Dies* (bypassing pay TV, cable and satellite) and its reruns of the previous 17 films have proved the only consistent ratings hit after the removal of *News At Ten*.

But back to those problems. Although Michael Apted got an early shot of the museum in the sun, it subsequently refused to shimmer. So it was Adrian Biddle's job to add a little internal luminescence to Gehry's titanium.

Another problem was that what did shimmer was approximately 100,000 Spaniards who had come to see the shoot, suffocating the streets, overloading apartment balconies and hanging from office windows. However, this was a pleasing problem, causing only a couple of hours' delay to rope off areas to make sure the shots were clean.

To those who were born at the time, it was like Beatlemania all over again – something that burst on the world 27 years previously at exactly the same time as the first Bond film, *Dr No*, in 1962. Brosnan was mobbed as few stars had been before. 'I was blown away,' he confessed. 'It was amazing. Gobstoppingly wonderful.'

The Bilbao trip was in January, early in the shoot, and such an overwhelming reaction from a non-English-speaking territory to the presence of a Bond film in town had a galvanizing effect on the crew's morale.

The exterior scene was Bond (Pierce to begin with, Mark Mottram later) jumping down 20 floors from an office building with the help of a curtain sash cord, with the Guggenheim in the background. As Michael Apted said: 'This is where we tell people, "You are in a Bond movie" within one and a half minutes of sitting down. The stunts are real. This is our signature.'

At the same time Apted found himself a little intimidated by the reception. 'This is our audience and they have pretty high standards. I've got to deliver what they want and more than they want. It's almost unnerving that there's so much expectation about the film.'

Unknown at the time to Apted or his team, they would return to two more locations in Spain as a substitute for Kazakhstan and the Caucasus Mountains. Even those were to create problems. The first was the exterior entrance to the nuclear facility, which was going to undergo a certain amount of gunfire and explosions. The Spanish lady who agreed to lease her territory north of Zaragoza to the company later changed her mind because she said the bangs would upset the baby eagles nearby. When it was pointed out to her that NATO planes zapped missiles into the selfsame mountain range every morning, she replied on behalf of the eaglets: 'Oh, they're used to that.'

The rain in Spain.

An alternative location was found in the nearby Bardenas Reales, near Tudela. This was Don Quixote country – the crew passed windmills on their journey from Zaragoza in the morning – and George Orwell country – nearly every town had its own bullring on the route to Pamplona.

Michael Wilson had few qualms about the audience being short-changed by the film's use of Spain to depict more easterly locations. 'They always used to say in Hollywood that once you got out into the desert, a rock is a rock and a tree is a tree.'

Denise in Spain.

In fact the art and special-effects departments had constructed a large and combustible military entrance to the table-topped mountain that housed the web of underground nuclear tunnels. Apted had shot the interiors of Bond's fight with Renard and his men over the past weeks on the 007 Stage at Pinewood. I was surprised at rushes one lunchtime to see Pierce actually catch fire and roll away from gunfire in a blazing boiler suit. I asked him about it that afternoon and he was rather proud: 'It could have been doubled but I felt pretty comfortable about it. There's been a lot of hanging on to wires and going down tubes with 600lb of gasoline going up your backside. "In for a penny, in for a pound" has been the motto on this one.'

Simon Crane had done a test on the shot himself without any protective clothing before letting Pierce do it wearing anti-fire Nemex underwear next to his skin – the kind Grand Prix drivers use. In Spain Pierce and Denise Richards had to emerge from the fireball tunnel with a torrent of flames behind them. This time Mark Mottram and Jo McClaren did double them for the wide angle. On the first take the flames shot only about 25 feet into the air, singeing their heels as they emerged from a sort of manhole cover. Both volunteered to do it again. The special-effects crew increased the petrol and isopropanol mixture by 150 per cent and an 80-foot pillar of flame nearly barbecued them as they leapt out of the hole.

Mark, since he was wearing Nemex, cleverly interposed his body between Jo and the fire. She was in Denise's skimpy outfit of vest and shorts and was thus unable to wear any protection save Zelgel, which is becoming more and more favoured as an anti-burn device. As Simon Crane said: 'It's safer and you don't look like the Michelin man.'

Jo McClaren, at only 27, has been in more movies than you might have noticed. She stunt-doubled Kate Blanchett in *Elizabeth*, was a

Stunt doubles Jo McClaren and Mark Mottram escape the pillar of flame.

female pilot in the latest Star Wars movie, *The Phantom Menace*, did all Rachel Weisz's stunts throughout *The Mummy* and now was stunt-doubling Denise, Sophie Marceau and even the Cigar Girl when Gary Powell barrel-rolled over her on the river.

Jo, a pretty, wide-faced girl with a shapely rather than athletic figure, passed three A-levels and studied at LAMDA, intent on a career in the theatre. In fact she spent a season at Leatherhead Rep, where she got her Equity card, but in her spare time worked on the six basic skills necessary for a career in stunts. You can tell why she has got to the top in her field: the agility and the guts almost go without saying, but what is just as important is a low-key attitude and a sang-froid that is quietly modest rather than modern-cool.

Chris Corbould had only one shot at blowing up his nuclear facility. A Spanish Air Force F16 Freedom Fighter had to fly through frame with the escaping Renard on board at the exact moment of a huge explosion that scattered an entire camp – Kazakhstan soldiers, a fleet of cars and trucks, International Decommissioning Agency scientists and technicians and local labour – into the desert. To ensure that no one would be hurt, Corbould had videoed tests with the same amount of explosives – 250 gallons of petrol and isopropanol and just over 30lb of gelignite – and then doubled the distance of the nearest object that was hit in the knowledge that heat goes further than flying debris. He had been rehearsing it all week.

More than the 100-degree heat was making the sweat stand out on Corbould's brow as he summoned in the Maltese pilots to make the crucial fly-past after a couple of test runs at just 50 feet above the ground and his assistant director rehearsed the ground action to make sure everybody could get clear of the fire and flying rubble in time.

Stunt men were closest to the explosion, with extras on foot and in vehicles in the next rank. Pierce and Denise were some 450 yards away in the foreground of the shot, while the pilot was guided in on constant radio talkback. All three were in alignment for less than a second, and then WHOOSH-BANG-KERPANG! Spot on. The heat of the explosion radiated miles, bouncing back off the mountain. Even the baby eagles must have looked up.

Mission accomplished, the unit moved four hours south to Los Callejones, near Cuenca, where a picturesque Turkish village, Coptic church and pipeline site miraculously emerged.

Michael Apted, John Richardson and Vic Armstrong.

The main problem for the conclusion of the movie was to tip over a nuclear submarine and slam it head first into the bed of the Bosporus – something never seen in a movie before. The underwater sequences were taken care of by the miniature-effects supervisor, JOHN RICHARDSON, who had supervised the visual effects and model-unit sequences on seven previous Bonds, starting with *Moonraker,* and whose film-industry pedigree is such that his father supervised the special effects on *Lawrence Of Arabia.*

Anthony Waye had built up a good relationship with the Royal Navy thanks to its participation in *Tomorrow Never Dies* – in fact a naval charity had been a beneficiary of the première. So his people were able to go and scrutinize a nuclear submarine to see how to build their own.

There was no question of ever using the real thing. A 45-foot model was built for the underwater sequences. And there was no question of using the Bosporus – apart from anything else it was too dark down at the bottom to see anything. So John Richardson had the penance of taking his sub and his crew of 12 to the Bahamas, where the deep water was clear enough to film in and warm enough to work in. Even so, when his underwater crew was shooting at their maximum depth of 100 feet they could stay under for no more than 19 minutes a day, breathing a Nitrox mixture, without the danger of decompression. At 80 feet underwater they found the current incredibly strong and the model very difficult to manoeuvre.

Everybody in Richardson's crew was trained in diving but there was also the small matter of sharks. The rule was to keep very still when they came to inspect the submarine and discover that it was not, in fact, one of their relations. The penultimate moment of the film is when the tail section of the submarine explodes. Richardson took three tails with him but managed to get the shot in his first take.

Other Richardson model moments which will only be considered to have succeeded if they are unnoticed are hot-air balloons (the wind will never let real ones stay still for repeated takes); helicopters (you can't blow up real helicopters in the air for movies); the pipeline construction sight with its own trees and snowy mountains built to scale; the BMW driving through the walkways (the car company lent him a model BMW which he rebuilt for his purposes); the destruction of the walkways set; the explosion in MI6; and the top of the Millennium Dome.

For the interior of the submarine, two matching full-scale sections – each consisting of the control room, the reactor, the machine room and the torpedo room – were built on A and D Stages. In this operation the storyboards were vital as actors and stunt men alternated between the two units working on them. Chris Corbould took advice from a specialist hydraulic company before assembling a sturdy 80-foot rig

Model pipeline.

with main beams that could lift up the submarine, move it through 90 degrees and then plunge it into a specially built tank in the studio floor.

We could only give the appearance of filling up the control room by dropping the whole set into the tank, because you could never get enough water physically pumping in and the logistics of making it watertight so that you could pump it in would be mind-blowing. The whole rig had to drop 12 feet vertically. There was a lot of stress and strain on the rig, so we had to allow a lot of grid in there to allow for free flow of water. It was more critical when we brought it out as you had ten feet of water inside the set and you had to bring it out very slowly after each take so that we wouldn't pull bits off the set.

On D Stage stunt men dropped like flies as the sub plunged into the seabed (most of the men had had a decent rehearsal for this on *Titanic*), while on A Stage Brosnan and Carlyle rejected safety wires as they engaged in a swashbuckling fight all over the vertical submarine. At the climax, the plutonium rod brought death to the vanquished – although not in the way intended.

Bond films are rich in unsung heroes whose work will only be considered perfect if it goes unnoticed. And heroines. MARA BRYAN is the visual-effects supervisor. Despite the Bond ethic that you do things for real where possible, with stunt men where not possible and with models where there are territories that even stunt men can't go, there are still some shots that can be generated only by computer. There are more than 200 of them in *Tomorrow Never Dies*, although few in the audience will have spotted more than a dozen. When actors are working very close to helicopter blades, the blades are nearly always put in later by the computer.

So, in the walkways scene, when the helicopter explodes and the flying blades come bouncing after Robbie Coltrane, on one angle at least the most modern form of screen technology is employed.

Mara Bryan.

To make a CGI version of a parahawk the machine itself is digitized. First it is covered with a mesh or grid moulded to the shape of the object with more intersections on the grid in areas of greatest detail. A visual-effects specialist takes a computer wand to it. The first point he picks is called zero. That becomes the scanner's reference point in space. From then on, every time the scanner moves, it knows where it is in relation to that point, so that as the technician digitizes point after point, he starts to build up a map which you can see on the computer as he covers all the intersections on the surface.

So one of those parahawks in one of those shots is not going to be real. Which one? Mara Bryan is determined no one will spot it:

The Sub on Stage D.

We want it to be absolutely accurate. It was never built with this in mind and the curves on the parahawk are really quite complex and we have to cut in directly with the real thing. We went to a tremendous amount of trouble to take reference video footage and stills of the real one on location to get the lighting right. I'm absolutely determined that they're going to be photo-real and there's no way you'll tell the difference.

Then – BLAM! – two of the parahawks explode into flames, and it may be just be possible to divine retrospectively which ones were Mara's.

Miss Bryan also adds the flames to gunshots – 'once in a while,' she admits. 'That's something that usually emerges afterwards.

Prototype parahawk.

Parahawk disaster.

Sometimes, on a particular take that the editor wants to use, the shutter misses the gun flash and they will asks us to put one in, but most of the time they'll get it for real.'

The guns, as ever, were provided by Charlie Bodycomb of Bapty and Co. Since the Dunblane tragedy ownership of handguns has been prohibited and Home Office Section Five authority was required to provide Bond with his Walther P99, Robbie Coltrane with his Heckler & Koch MP5K, Sophie with her Colt 45 1911 H1 and Bobby Carlyle with his Sig P229 – all real guns carefully customized by Bapty and Co. to fire blanks.

But enough about the violence – what about the sex? It was a subject I felt slightly uncomfortable about discussing with Pierce. 'How do you justify in these politically correct times that Bond still ... er?' I asked.

'That he still likes bonking women?' he finished my sentence for me. 'Bonking and Bond go hand in hand. In all, I think we've got a fair plethora of girls in this to please any male out there from 12 to 112. I suppose he's not lathered in babes as he used to be – which would be a bit naff now. We'd be touching the world of Austin Powers if we did that.'

I made the female body count three during the shooting. First to fall was Dr Molly Warmflash, while Bond was trying to demonstrate to her that he should get a clean bill of health after his nasty knock on the Dome.

The very thought of the name proved alluring to Serena Scott Thomas. 'I couldn't resist Dr Molly Warmflash. I had never met Pierce before and we did a love scene on the first day. There I was, thrown in at the deep end.'

That was in an icy castle in Scotland. The film concludes in warmer climes with Bond and Dr Christmas Jones on a chaise longue on a romantic balcony in Istanbul. This was something Denise Richards, Starship Trooper, took in her stride. 'We had no discussion about it. We rehearsed it. We were both very comfortable with what we were doing. It's a PG film, so there were no worries about what the audience might see – and we just did it.'

These are close encounters of the flirt kind. More substantial is Bond's entanglement with Sophie Marceau's Elektra King. This provided director Michael Apted with problems:

I did 16 takes on the scene when they're making love, largely because I couldn't shoot a nipple. About ten of those 16 takes I can't use because they have nipples in them. That's the kind of absurd limitation we have in order to get a PG certificate. You can show people blowing each other's brains out in one part of the film but you can't show a nipple in the other half.

We rehearsed the scene for 20 minutes at about eight in the morning, which is not the easiest time. He likes her for a start – that's a terrific bonus. We didn't want to do the same old stuff. I'd had the idea of using ice and Sophie developed the thing of kissing him with the ice. She's really good to work with because she's uninhibited.

'If there is no love story in the film,' Sophie Marceau observed, 'there's something missing. Bond and Elektra like each other, they play with each other. Sex exists. A Bond film is a totally abstract world and if you're Bond you meet women. A film has to be seductive. The film business is about sex – the business is seduction.'

And the ice? 'A love scene is the situation it is in. You have to tell the story of the scene. It can be hot and steamy if it happens in a sauna,' Sophie told me with a smile.

"How was I?"

CHAPTER NINE

THANK Q

Filming is coming to an end. I'm having a chat with Pierce one morning and, not really expecting a direct reply, casually ask him if there's any part of a Bond shoot that he particularly looks forward to doing. His reply was unhesitating: 'Q is top of the list.'

The scene in which Bond is given the latest MI6 gadgetry which will save him in his hour of need is always put at the end of the shooting schedule. The reason is simple. During the film Bond may have used many devices, some of which will have landed up on the cutting room floor because they didn't prove wholly effective or for reasons of length. So the meeting in which Bond is instructed in and equipped with his invaluable lifesavers is logically shot when the film-makers already know which ones he is going to use.

It was an especially poignant scene in *The World Is Not Enough* as Q, played by Desmond Llewelyn, tells Bond he is planning for his retirement. Llewelyn first appeared in *From Russia With Love* 36 years ago and has been in 17 of the 19 Bond films.

Not that he was thinking of retiring – although 85 is a little over the usual Civil Service retirement age – but rather he was concerned that he might not be active enough for the next movie in three years' time. However, he resolutely assured me: 'I will be in the Bond films as long as the producers want me and the Almighty doesn't.'

But, some time before, he had informed the producers that he might not be able to do *The World Is Not Enough* as he was due to go into hospital for an operation and suggested that maybe he should have an assistant so that, either way, the scenes could be covered.

And this is where I played a small part in the Bond story. During the time I spent writing *Fierce Creatures* with John Cleese, we talked a great deal about cinema and he frequently expressed the desire to

play a Bond villain. John would sit in his winged chair in his study stroking one of his beloved cats, usually Ronnie or Reggie, and utter in a chilling tone: 'I've been expecting you, Mr Bond.'

He pointed out: 'I always think the villains have the best roles. Everyone's said that. Even theologians have said the devil has all the best jokes. Playing something evil is so much more fun, particularly if the evil person has a little bit of humour. The only Shakespeare I ever saw when I was young was Olivier's *Richard III* and I loved it.'

At the same time I did a job for Barbara Broccoli and Michael Wilson: presenting the Celebration of the Life and Work of Cubby Broccoli at the Odeon, Leicester Square, in November 1996. In the discussions we had about the ceremony I let drop the information that

my writing partner had a yen to be a Bond villain. Barbara and Michael were intrigued though noncommittal. They certainly liked John's work. But during further discussion of the possibility they felt that his comedic persona was so strong that it would overwhelm the necessary demonic quality of the part.

Subsequently Desmond informed them he might have to step down. I was watching a screening of William Nicholson's *Firelight* at the Eon viewing theatre in Piccadilly, where Michael Apted and Michael Wilson were looking at Sophie Marceau as a possible villain. 'Can she deliver Europe?' Michael Wilson asked slightly wryly afterwards, knowing that MGM/UA in Hollywood were pushing for an American actress.

Afterwards I had dinner with him and his wife Jane, and he reminded me that I had told him that John Cleese was interested in the Bond films and gently enquired whether he would be at all interested in the role of Q if Desmond proved unavailable.

John was in Santa Barbara in California when I sounded him out later that night. He wasn't too keen – Bond was shooting in January and he hated the English winter. I talked further with Michael, who made the offer more attractive by guaranteeing a role in *The World Is*

Q-glasses.

Not Enough for John, plus an option to appear in three more Bonds –
which meant ten years of international screen prominence.

This seemed a better offer for the British actor. John became much
more interested, always provided the winter shoot could be kept to a
minimum. His agents were contacted and a deal was struck.

Few people – including the producers Cubby Broccoli and
Harry Saltzman – realized that the reason Q was called Q was that it
was short for Quartermaster. MI6 adopted the army term for the
officer who distributes equipment to the troops. The part has a
history that goes back to the Fleming novels. When he had
published a couple, the author got a letter from a Major Boothroyd
in Glasgow commending him on his plots but condemning him for
his 'deplorable taste in weapons'. The Major pointed out that the
Biretta was a fairly feckless gun and tended to be kept by ladies in
their handbags.

Fleming loved this and not only incorporated the information
in *Dr No* but also put in a character called Major Boothroyd as
the MI6 armourer who hands Bond a Walther PPK. Peter Burton,
who played the part in the 1962 film, was unavailable to appear
in *From Russia With Love* the next year, so Desmond Llewelyn
became Boothroyd, whom M describes as being from Q
branch. Boothroyd gives Bond an attaché case full of handy
gadgets, not the least handy feature of which is the fact that
the case itself will explode in your face if you open it the
wrong way.

An early script for *Goldfinger* (1964) contained the separate
characters of Q and Boothroyd, but Llewelyn pointed out to the
producers that they were one and the same man. Thus he immortalized himself as Q, not least by presenting James Bond with the
legendary Aston Martin DB5 with an ejector seat.

It was Guy Hamilton, the director of *Goldfinger*, who gave Llewelyn a hook on the character, as Llewelyn recalled:

I was working at my desk in MI6, and James Bond came in and I got up to greet him. But Guy said: 'No, no, don't take any notice of this man.' I was slightly surprised and I replied: 'But this is James Bond.' And Guy pointed out: 'He doesn't treat your gadgets with the right respect, so you don't like him at all.' This gave me the clue straight away. However, over the years Q has become extremely fond of Bond, but he disagrees with the girls and all the carrying on.

In *The World Is Not Enough*, for the first time in 19 movies, Bond helps himself to a piece of Q's equipment without permission and streaks up the Thames in the jet boat in pursuit of the Cigar Girl. Q's remonstration that this was a 'fishing boat' that he had been intending for his retirement may, as I noted earlier, be interpreted by cineastes in years to come as a slightly tongue-in-cheek telling off.

Nevertheless, Q and R equip 007 with, among other wizardry, glasses that will enable him to see though crooks' clothes to discover if they are armed in the Baku casino; a coat that will inflate into a balloon if he finds himself caught in an avalanche; and a BMW with missiles to shoot down helicopters should the need arise.

The word 'wizard' was uppermost in Bruce Feirstein's mind when he wrote the possible parting of the ways heralded by Q's talk of retirement:

I had lunch with Desmond and he said, 'You've got to find a way to write me out of this with dignity and style.' After working on two Bonds he was a character who meant a lot to me. It occurred to me that here you were dealing with Merlin and Arthur saying goodbye – Q's Merlin to Bond's

Arthur. The two men face each other. Bond fights back any sentimentality and kinds of hesitates. He just says 'Well' – in parenthesis it says, 'Will I see you again?' You don't want him to say that but you want him to imply it. Q comes back just with business. 'Pay attention, 007. There are two things I've always tried to teach you.'

Now in the initial draft the first thing he said was: 'Never comfort the enemy', but Michael Wilson thought this wasn't strong enough. We were reading it through on the set of the casino scene and Michael said: 'Isn't there some expression about there being three rules in life like – never check your baggage, never do something else and never let them see you bleed?' And I said: 'That's the line' – and it's in the script.'

Q's second piece of advice is simply: 'Always have an escape plan' and with that he simply disappears, giving Desmond Llewelyn a gracious though not necessarily final exit. Not that Desmond will ever disappear. Not only does he have 17 films under his belt, but in the 007 Licence to Thrill Rides (in Paramount theme parks across America and in the Trocadero Centre in Piccadilly Circus) Q's lab provides aspiring agents with exploding alarm clocks and toothpaste tubes, a watch that can detonate a mine, a Lotus Esprit from *The Spy Who Loved Me* and the Acrostar Jet from *Octopussy*.

Q leads the assault on writer Bruce Feirstein.

POSTSCRIPT

The Bond books were written for adults and the early films certainly had a sophistication to them that appealed to, say, the Playboy generation. But Bond has now reached down and scooped up the children's market, as is evidenced by the huge success of the Nintendo GoldenEye 007 game in which the pre-teens can bungee-jump, stick mines on tanks and tracker bugs on helicopters, shoot their way out of tight situations and bring Alec Trevelyan (renegade agent 006) to book.

Does such a game ignite violence in young souls? Yes, a bit, I should have thought, but no more than a daily diet of television or a game of Cowboys and Indians in the park.

Bond is now a man for all seasons and all generations. It's hard to institutionalize an institution, but with Brosnan the Broccoli family seems to have managed it. Having observed Brigadier Apted and his forces in action, I could see that the sheer sense of competition between separate divisions to get their work in the final cut was enough to ensure the highest standards.

But at Divisional Headquarters there were always minds at work making sure that the shock of the new remains true to the tradition of the past. Everybody is inputting ideas to Michael Wilson and Barbara Broccoli the whole time. In the case of the glasses that see through clothes in the casino scene, a storyboard artist had come up with the original idea that they would reveal one woman in the room to be a transvestite. But Michael Wilson nixed the notion:

It was gross. It was just one of a hundred little things that Barbara and I run around trying to adjust. I guess I came on board when MGM had a policy of hiring great film-makers like Woody Allen, Norman Jewison, the Mirisch brothers – and letting them make the films they thought were interesting. That's what we try to do. We listen to the audience. But we don't keep

testing our films to research what an audience want to see. I think that's totally preposterous, because if you give an audience what they want to see, you'll find it's so predictable they don't like it.

Barbara Broccoli was born and bred on the Bond films. Her presence on the set can sometimes seem invisible but her input is there to be seen in the final product. When Bond appears to be about to kill the unarmed Renard in *The World Is Not Enough* there was a feeling that he needed a line to accompany his action. 'Fleming always used to say, "Cold-blooded murder is a filthy business,"' Barbara mentioned casually.

It's up there – on the screen. That is precisely what Bond now says. The extraordinary thing about a Bond film is though it is light-hearted in content – few modern movies are quite as escapist – this light touch is achieved with as serious and dedicated professionalism as you would find on the set of a Spielberg or Bergman film. Things don't happen by accident; they happen because seasoned experts know what is right.

FILM CREDITS

THE CREW

Producers	MICHAEL G. WILSON
	BARBARA BROCCOLI
Director	MICHAEL APTED
Screenplay	NEAL PURVIS &
	ROBERT WADE
Line Producer	ANTHONY WAYE
Production Designer	PETER LAMONT
Director of Photography	ADRIAN BIDDLE
Editor	JIM CLARK
Costume Designer	LINDY HEMMING
2nd Unit Director	VIC ARMSTRONG
Stunt Co-Ordinator	SIMON CRANE
Special Effects Supervisor	CHRIS CORBOULD
Casting	DEBBIE McWILLIAMS
Visual Effects Supervisor	MARA BRYAN
Miniature Effects Supervisor	JOHN RICHARDSON
3rd Unit Director	ARTHUR WOOSTER
Aerial Co-Ordinator	MARC WOLFF
2nd Unit Cameraman	JONATHAN TAYLOR
Director of Publicity	ANNE BENNETT
Stills Photographer	KEITH HAMPSHIRE
Chief Electrician	KEVIN DAY
Hair Supervisor	COLIN JAMISON
Make-up Supervisor	LINDA DE VETTA
Production Supervisor	JANINE MODDER
Production Supervisor (Azerbaijan)	HUGH HARLOW
Production Supervisor (Turkey)	PHILIP KOHLER
Sound Recordist	CHRIS MUNRO
Script Supervisor	NIKKI CLAPP
Assistant Director	GERRY GAVIGAN
2nd Assistant Director	TERRY MADDEN
Financial Controller	ANDREW NOAKES
Associate Producer	NIGEL GOLDSACK
Construction Co-Ordinator	PETER G. WILLIAMS
Mr. Brosnan's Make-Up Artist	BRON ROYLANCE
Mr. Brosnan's Hairdresser	RICK PROVENZANO
Unit Publicist	GEOFF FREEMAN
Music	DAVID ARNOLD
The World is Not Enough Performed by	GARBAGE

THE CAST

James Bond	PIERCE BROSNAN
Elektra King	SOPHIE MARCEAU
Renard	ROBERT CARLYLE
Christmas Jones	DENISE RICHARDS
Valentin Zukovsky	ROBBIE COLTRANE
M	JUDI DENCH
Q	DESMOND LLEWELYN
Q's Assistant	JOHN CLEESE
Moneypenny	SAMANTHA BOND
Sir Robert King	DAVID CALDER
Tanner	MICHAEL KITCHEN
Robinson	COLIN SALMON
Doctor Molly Warmflash	SERENA SCOTT THOMAS
Gabor	JOHN SERU
Colonel Akakievich	CLAUDE-OLIVER RUDOLPH
Davidov	ULRICH THOMSEN
The Bull	GOLDIE
Cigar Girl	MARIA GRAZIA CUCINOTTA
Lachaise	PATRICK MALAHIDE
Coptic Priest	DIRAN MEGHREBLIAN